Pre-Roman Britain

PRE-ROMAN

Stanley Thomas

BRITAIN

New York Graphic Society Publishers, Ltd

Greenwich, Connecticut 06831

© Stanley Thomas 1965
Published 1965 by Studio Vista Limited, London, England
First published in the United States of America in 1966
by New York Graphic Society Publishers, Limited
Library of Congress Catalog Card Number 65-23597
Set in 13 pt Bembo
Printed and bound in Great Britain by
R & R Clark Limited, Edinburgh, Scotland

Contents

Preface

This book aims at providing a visual account of the works of prehistoric man in Britain. This new form of presentation will, it is hoped, satisfy some of the needs of the ever-growing archaeological public not already met by existing works, and enable students to gain a wider acquaintance with monuments and museum objects than would otherwise be possible without a great deal of travelling. Although there cannot be any satisfactory substitute for the actual handling of specimens, the opportunities for such experience will always be limited for the general public, and the photographs are intended to offer a second-best alternative by trying to give some feeling of scale, mass and texture. It has not been possible, in the text and captions, to enter into the important and fundamental arguments in which prehistorians are currently engaged, but I have given what I believe to be a generally acceptable picture, even if it shows some personal bias. Many of my statements ought properly to be accompanied by constant qualification, but I have deliberately avoided the tedious repetition of such words as 'possibly', 'perhaps', etc., except where they seemed inescapable.

In such a book I cannot but be deeply indebted to my teachers and colleagues, and not least to former and present students, both adult and undergraduate. To all of these I offer my thanks and ask their indulgence for not mentioning them all by name. Nor do I intend any discourtesy in thanking all together the many individuals and institutions who have provided me with photographs, even when I could not include them for reasons outside my control; their names appear in the list of acknowledgements, and I hope they will accept this as a personal message of gratitude for their kind help. I am also deeply grateful to the Directors, Keepers, Curators and staffs of the museums where I was welcomed to take up their time and disturb their displays in order to photograph items from their collections; the list of such museums is similarly intended as an individual expression of my indebtedness to each.

Of certain individuals I must make personal mention. First, the very writing of the book is due to my friend, Professor Richard Atkinson, and his wife, Hester; I wish I could do more than this to recompense their inspiration and constant help. Next, to Mr Malcolm Murray of the Department of Prehistoric Archaeology, Edinburgh University, I owe all the excellent photographs of material from Scotland; for this and the great influence that his photographic techniques have had on my own, I am most grateful. My colleague, Mr Derek Simpson, Mr A. L. Pacitto, Archaeological Technician at

Leicester University, and I formed the team responsible for many of the photographs from English museums; I would thank them most warmly for their great labours, often undertaken under conditions of severe hardship. I also acknowledge my indebtedness to Mr Michael Sissons of A. D. Peters and to Mr Robert Cross, Miss Gillian Greenwood and Mr Robin Wright of Studio Vista Ltd, who have shown understanding and patience in seeing this book to its completion.

Finally, I welcome this opportunity of expressing my heartfelt thanks to four individuals who alone know how heavy a debt I owe them: to Jack Simmons who, despite his own great burdens of work and worry, has never failed to give encouragement and wise counsel, and to my wife and children, who bore ungrudgingly the domestic repercussions of this undertaking and helped me to take many of the photographs.

Any virtues that the book may have are largely due to those I have mentioned; its faults lie in me.

STANLEY THOMAS

LEICESTER UNIVERSITY
October, 1964

Introduction

Man, in the evolved form in which he exists today, displays a great many fundamental differences, of both degree and kind, from the rest of the animal kingdom. He walks erect, his arms and hands remaining free for other purposes, especially for grasping by opposing his thumb and fingers; he manufactures tools, not merely uses them, and relies on manufactured equipment and mental agility for his personal survival and for securing food, instead of on physical strength, size, speed or specialized bodily features. He is a rational being, able to formulate abstract ideas which he can also communicate by means of articulate speech, and has thus built up through the ages an accumulated body of tradition, transmitted from generation to generation. And finally he is a spiritual being, possessing or claiming to possess some kind of eternal, non-physical existence—a soul.

By means of all these characteristic faculties—physical, intellectual and spiritual—Man has gradually evolved a series of highly intricate and sophisticated societies, a vast heritage of technical, philosophical, religious and artistic traditions, and an immense range of material structures and equipment. The history of human culture has been stimulated and moulded not only by geography and natural environment which determine the pattern of all animal life, but also by social, political and religious factors, the structure and organization of society itself, and not least by the character and personalities of particular individuals. It is the task of the historian to piece together and interpret the development and growth of such societies, but the prehistorian, concerned with periods and peoples for whom no written evidence survives to throw light on thoughts, motives and events, has to contend with very special problems in the search for his basic information.

First, it is almost impossible now to visualize the way of life and the conceptual world of the earliest creatures who link Man with his purely animal ancestors, or to grasp the reality of the hundreds of thousands of years of almost imperceptible change that represent the first steps in human history. Our studies must go back to the very humblest beginnings, when the characteristic human faculties first appeared and had their initial growth, and to times when human development, though rapid and indeed explosive by geological and evolutionary time-scales, was immeasurably slow by comparison with more recent advances. Secondly, the volume of surviving evidence is treacherously small. Man was at first a very rare animal and we have only the scantiest and most haphazard record of his skeletal remains during those long ages when he was becoming distinguished physically from the higher apes. His earliest attempts at tool-making are quite impossible to identify unless they are found with his skeletal remains or in undoubted dwelling sites, and such conditions are exceptionally rare. Even when easily identifiable tools were being made, little survives except tools or tool parts of stone and metal and sometimes the bones of men and animals. And thirdly, we can hardly hope, from these few fragmentary remains, to recover anything but a distorted picture of human activities or to study more than a very restricted range of the innumerable facets of life. Even the picture that builds up in our imagination will be biased by our modern surroundings, traditions and mental processes. In particular, we are liable to seek too simple a pattern of life and too uniform a sequence of development, while the true picture should be one of countless threads, some continuous and others broken, of success and failure, isolation and fusion.

Nevertheless, always bearing in mind the limitations of both our evidence and our chances of interpreting it correctly, we can begin to outline in the broadest terms the story of human development and achievement, at least in material things, from the earliest beginnings up to the time when written records survive to give us a more intimate knowledge of human actions and thoughts.

Our earliest ancestors

Lower Palaeolithic (Earlier Old Stone Age) 500,000–60,000 BC

It was apparently not in Europe, but in the warmer lands further south, that Man originally emerged as a distinct group among the upper primates. The first unquestionable tool-making communities in Britain and on the mainland of the Continent (to which Britain was united throughout this period) have an antiquity of something like half a million years. There are more ancient flint objects that some scholars claim to have been deliberately fashioned, but there will always be controversy about them, since it is impossible to distinguish for certain between deliberate and natural origins until chipping techniques and the shapes of implements are completely distinctive and standardized. It is likely, however, that tool-using if not actual tool-making ancestors of our first identifiable Palaeolithic communities existed in Britain far back in time.

True tool-makers, then, colonized this country early in the Ice Age. Throughout the repeated cycles of climatic change that together make up this period we find traces of their occupation: probably not a continuous sequence, for in the colder phases they doubtless migrated south beyond the forbidding environments surrounding the ice-sheets, although the latter never completely covered the southern parts of Britain. In the warmer phases, however, when climatic conditions were sometimes more favourable than today, they returned as the herds of animals on which they lived and the vegetation which supported the herds recolonized the countryside.

The surviving traces of these peoples consist almost exclusively of flint and stone tools, the debris of their manufacture and bones of food animals. The tools (2-6) are of the simplest kind, being shaped from rough flakes struck from a nodule, or 'hand-axes' consisting of the nodules themselves, trimmed to shape by removing small chips from the surface. All were multi-purpose tools for cutting and shaping wood, killing and flaying animals, preparing skins, carving meat, digging for vegetable foods and other functions. Because of their very simplicity and multiple functions, such tools changed only very gradually during the enormously long period of hundreds of millennia. Improved techniques of flint working can be traced, however, both in the hand-axes, leading to finely shaped, elegant objects, and in the flake industries, most particularly in the production of more regular shapes. Indeed, by the end of this period we already find the beginning of specialized implements for particular purposes.

Different forms of human beings may have developed these two traditions—of flake tools and hand-axes together with small utilized flakes—or they may represent the same societies modifying their equipment to different environmental conditions. But we know little of the everyday life of the Lower Palaeolithic folk. They lived in small, family communities, scattered extremely thinly over the countryside, and constantly moving in pursuit of the wild game and seeking known areas of vegetable foods from season to season. Their shelters would have been of the humblest kind, and very few of their camp sites have survived because of the action of ice, water and soil during succeeding glacial phases. Those that do exist (3) were situated by former lakes or rivers, and yield concentrations of tools and the waste products of their manufacture; sometimes there are indications of burning, but not hearths, since Man could not yet control or make fire for protection, warmth or cooking. The animal bones show the changing faunal populations in the different climatic phases—from such species as cave lion, hippopotamus, elephant and rhinoceros in the warm interglacials, through temperate woodland forms such as red deer, elk, fallow deer, wild cattle, etc., to the steppe and tundra animals, horse, reindeer, woolly rhinoceros and mammoth of the glacial phases. Botanical evidence too, from pollen grains preserved in peats and clays, shows the cycle of vegetational changes during the interglacial periods as trees, grasses and other plants in turn colonized and disappeared from the countryside; and shows, indeed, some vegetational changes that might have been produced by the activities of Man himself.

Very few human skeletal remains have yet been recovered from this period in Britain, and there is nothing to suggest the existence here of any of the kinds of 'ape-man' or 'near-man' that are known in Africa and the Far East. Our earliest human remains, from the ancient Thames gravels at Swanscombe in Kent (2), are tantalizingly incomplete; they consist of the back parts of a skull which could equally well belong to an early form of the 'Neanderthal' family and thus link up with other remains from Europe, or lie in a direct ancestral line to true Modern Man, *Homo sapiens*. If the latter, they would be by far the earliest remains of Modern Man yet known.

Upper Palaeolithic (Later Old Stone Age) 60,000–10,000 BC

We know much more of the communities inhabiting Britain during the last cold phase of the Ice Age, and the picture that emerges is strikingly different. Unfortunately, the cultures that on the Continent represent the chronological link between the Lower and Upper Palaeolithic—those associated with evolved Neanderthal Man—occur only in the Channel Isles and, in a modified form, in the extreme south of England. For the rest, there is a sharp break between the two periods and the human races that characterize them, for the Upper Palaeolithic inhabitants of Britain, as of Europe, belong unquestionably to the family of Modern Man.

The first innovations of these cultures are their occupation of the mouths of caves (7, 8), where such existed, their ability to control and make fire, and the use of clothing, probably of animal fur and leather. All these factors made Man far better able to adapt himself to climatic change; he could now survive and flourish even through the arctic phases of a glacial period in northern latitudes. It is, incidentally, the use of caves that is responsible for the survival of a far wider range of Man's equipment leading to our greater knowledge of his way of life.

Technologically, the Upper Palaeolithic peoples were well in advance of their predecessors. In flint work they developed a wide range of specialist tools shaped from long, parallel-sided 'blades' whose production demands great technical skill. They also exploited the physical properties of bone, antler and ivory (as well as wood) for hafts, composite tools edged or tipped with flint, and a wide variety of implements and personal ornaments. Their hunting and fishing gear comprised the harpoon, spear and (probably) the bow and arrow, and their tools (9-12, 14) included scrapers, borers and eyed needles for making fur and leather garments and utensils, knife blades and carving tools (17) for working bone and antler and cutting sinews and meat, and different types of scraper probably for woodworking. Their appreciation and confident control of the raw materials at their disposal might be even more fully demonstrated if their leatherwork and woodwork had survived.

Economically the Upper Palaeolithic cultures were intimately adapted to their environment and apparently flourished and prospered in it. At the same time and doubtless because of this close adaptation, regional and chronological differences became more sharply accentuated and changes in material equipment more rapid, in striking contrast to the wide uniformity over enormous areas and immense periods of the Lower Palaeolithic cultures. The British groups, for example, were already diverging from and apparently less prosperous than their parent groups in Europe.

Among the most interesting characteristics of Upper Palaeolithic cultures are the appearance of personal ornaments and ceremonial or status symbols and the practice of magico-religious rites, including the careful burial of the dead. Animal teeth and bone objects were worn as bangles and necklaces (14), and the body and face may also have been tattooed and painted, such adornment distinguishing not only one social unit from another but also age, sex or status divisions within society. Perhaps the so-called '*bâtons-de-commandement*' (handled antler objects perforated at the broad end) (12) symbolized authority and status, although other more mundane functions have been postulated. The elaborate burial of the dead is illustrated in several caves in Britain; the skeletons were sometimes covered with a deposit of red ochre, possibly symbolizing the colour of blood, and might also be accompanied by personal ornaments and grave goods, including in one case a '*bâton*'. Meanwhile, the magico-religious concepts that are most vividly illustrated by the sculptures, paintings and engravings on cave walls and stone and bone equipment of contemporary peoples in France and Spain, are dimly reflected in the few minor engravings on bone that have so far been discovered in Britain (13, 15). Even these suffice to give a slight insight into the hunting magic ritual that was probably only one of the many religious practices pervading every thought and act of the Upper Palaeolithic communities.

Mesolithic (Middle Stone Age) 10,000–3000 BC

As the ice sheets of the last glacial period retreated and there began the warmer climatic phase in which we are still living, the landscape of Britain changed once again from a dwarf tundra and steppe vegetation, first to a birch-pine cover and then to heavy forest of oak, elm, lime and hazel. New animal populations followed and Man, too, modified his way of life, the siting of his habitations and his equipment in response to the fresh materials and new sources of food.

The Mesolithic peoples of Britain shared the same broad traditions as their contemporaries in various parts of Europe and, now, of Scandinavia as well. But they continued also to develop their own distinctive features, and even within this country we can trace several divergent regional groups. Those of whom we know most are the forest dwellers, engaged in hunting, fishing and fowling; even their equipment in such perishable materials as wood and bark as well as bone, antler and flint has occasionally survived in the peat deposits that formed in the beds of the lakes at whose edges they camped. Their hunting and fishing gear included pronged spears (18) and arrows, tipped or edged with the tiny, carefully shaped flint points (microliths) that are characteristic of most Mesolithic industries (20). But they also introduced two important new tools, the axe and the adze, with which to exploit their forest environment, making platforms of logs and brushwood for their dwelling sites, canoes with paddles for fishing and doubtless much else besides.

Other contemporary groups in Britain appear poverty-stricken by comparison, but this is due to the accident of survival, for only their flint equipment is known at present. Some, it is true, did not possess the axe and would therefore be adapted to a different way of life from the forest folk, and their distribution suggests that they preferred a different kind of terrain, in the acid soils of which only flintwork survives. Yet others, especially in Scotland, lack both the axe and the otherwise universal microliths, and these shore-dwellers would have subsisted on a variety of sea foods, especially shellfish, although their fine harpoons show that their diet included much larger creatures as well (21).

The flimsy, temporary dwellings of the Mesolithic folk have left scant trace. Even at Star Carr (16), where a lakeside platform has been discovered, nothing has remained of any shelters. Elsewhere, slight, scoop-like hollows with occupation debris probably represent hut floors covered by tent-like, oval or round shelters, perhaps roofed with thatch or skins. The small communities still moved seasonally from one site to another, following the natural habits of the wild game and the favourite habitats of vegetable foods—roots, fruits, berries and nuts.

Little is known of the physical form of the Mesolithic peoples of Britain; their use of open sites and perhaps a change in religious traditions have resulted in a complete absence of burials. The only evidence of their ritual practices consists of a number of deer skulls, perforated through the forehead and with the antlers hollowed out, which may have been worn for stalking deer or, more probably, on the heads of dancers in some magic hunting ceremony (19).

The separation of Britain from the mainland of Europe in about 6-5000 BC by the cutting of the Channel and the flooding by the North Sea of the great plain that linked eastern England with Scandinavia, resulted in an even greater isolation of the native Mesolithic cultures. We do not know for how long they continued to follow their traditional hunting and food-gathering activities, but it was probably for several centuries after the first arrival of new immigrants towards the end of the fourth millennium BC. These folk brought with them a totally different form of economy, material culture, burial rites and religion and introduced a quite new pattern of life into prehistoric Britain. But the native inhabitants were not superseded suddenly or wiped out; they were indeed to play an important part in the later development of the farming economy. Sometimes the two groups would live side by side with little impact on one another; sometimes there may have been conflict and elsewhere again they may quite quickly have fused. Future discoveries may demonstrate these relationships in different regions and show the extent of the survival of Mesolithic traditions.

Early farmers and metalworkers

Earlier Neolithic (New Stone Age) 3500/3000–2100 BC

The settlement pattern of the earlier Neolithic communities is a complex one, made up of a large number of small units, some consisting of bands of immigrants, others representing the progressive fusion of these with the native Mesolithic peoples. The main distinguishing features of these different units lie in the form and decoration of their pottery, now manufactured for the first time in Britain, from which it is possible to establish broad regional groupings, chronological phases and continental origins. In addition our evidence now derives not only from settlements but also from burials and other more specialized kinds of site, even though difficulties arise when we try to correlate these with pottery groupings and with one another.

First, and beginning earliest, are groups of colonists who infiltrated over a long period from different areas, predominantly in France. They brought plain pottery vessels with simple, bag-like shapes of 'Western Neolithic' type (25), as well as their seed grain and domestic animals. Secondly, starting somewhat later but continuing their immigrations side by side with later groups of western folk, are communities whose 'Derivative' pottery styles show affinities with many different areas, some in the west but others from further east on the Continent, perhaps as far as Belgium and north Germany (26, 27). These, too, were farming folk who helped to consolidate the new economy in Britain, and it is perhaps to them we should attribute the special technique of forest clearance by burning. Thirdly, closely allied to the second groups and possibly representing their intermingling with the aboriginal Mesolithic communities, we may distinguish the beginnings of an 'Insular Neolithic' tradition (78, 79). Finally, in the west and north of Britain, numerous burial monuments betoken the establishment of local Neolithic colonies, whose relationship to the settlers in lowland Britain is still obscure (28). These 'Megalithic' elements first arrived during the earlier Neolithic, some perhaps as early as any of the colonies in southern England.

We cannot examine here the ultimate origins and early spread of farming in the Near and Middle East; but by the time cereal cultivation and animal husbandry reached Britain, the methods employed in each had undergone successive modification in the different environments through which they had passed across Europe. The staple grain was wheat, and the farmers preferred to cultivate light soils carrying thin woodland cover, just such land as would be found on the chalk downlands of Sussex and Wessex and probably in some river gravel areas as well. The preparation of the ground consisted of cutting down the branches and tops of the trunks of the trees and burning them and the undergrowth to provide a clearing and fertilize the soil; after a few harvests, when the heart went out of the soil, the patch would be abandoned and the cycle repeated in a fresh one. There were thus no true fields, nor was any other equipment required than the hoe and rake. Such methods were extremely wasteful and hazardous, and since there must have been many harvest failures for this and other reasons, one might expect a gradual decline in this branch of farming.

Stock-breeding provided a more reliable source of food, and always accompanied cereal production in the Neolithic farming economy, although the relative importance of one to the other is difficult to estimate. Cattle predominated among the livestock, with some sheep, goats and swine, their mutual proportions doubtless depending on local environments and traditions. One of the more spectacular classes of field monument built by the earlier Neolithic farmers in southern England—the 'causewayed camps'— should be associated with their animal husbandry (22, 23), for these must owe their size of up to about twenty acres to the need for enclosing flocks and herds. The camps comprise one or more rings of palisaded banks thrown up from discontinuous quarry ditches and, in addition to the mustering, sorting, branding, sale and slaughter of the livestock, may also have provided the sites for fairs and general barter sales and various social and religious activities. An expansion of stock-breeding at the expense of cereal production seems to have occurred during this period, and such a trend would be accentuated as the Mesolithic communities became absorbed into the farming economy; they may indeed have begun to protect and even rear their own animals before the Neolithic colonization, and would have been more sympathetically inclined to the keeping of livestock than to land cultivation.

The two main food-producing activities were supplemented by hunting, fishing and fowling, the extent of these depending on local conditions and seasonal shortages. Finely made leaf-shaped arrowheads are indeed characteristic of the Neolithic farmers and recent discoveries of Neolithic material include fragments of long bows (41-45). Once again the progressive infusion of Mesolithic elements into the Neolithic communities would tend to increase the scale of such activities in the later stages of the period (39, 40).

Only rare and scant traces survive of early Neolithic houses—small, rectangular buildings walled with clay and wattle on cobbled footings, with a ridged roof supported by internal posts and covered with thatch, reeds or turf (24). Domestic crafts included pottery making, leatherwork (31), carpentry, basketry and probably weaving and rope-making with vegetable fibres. Individual communities would be self-sufficient except for one important item, the axe (29, 30). For axe blades, either large nodules of first-class flint such as rarely occurred on the surface, or blocks of some other suitable hard rock were needed. To meet this demand there arose the oldest British industries: the mining and rough shaping of flint in East Anglia, Sussex and Wessex (32, 33), and somewhat later the working of fine-grained stone in such areas of highland Britain as the Lake District, Wales and Cornwall (34, 35). The specialist craftsmen who chipped their blocks into rough-outs for axes and traded them throughout the country for final grinding and polishing by the customer were the first classes or communities to be dependent for their livelihood on the barter of their products.

There is indirect evidence, too, for the development of other skills and mechanical principles. The megalithic tombs (see below) imply a knowledge of at least some elementary engineering principles and the ability to move and erect great masses of stone. Their builders, if not the other immigrants as well, were also experienced sailors with efficient sea-going vessels, in which they opened and maintained contact with the Atlantic coasts of western Europe and perhaps the Mediterranean. Wheeled vehicles, too, may already have been used in Britain, as they were in Neolithic times in the Low Countries whence some of our colonists may have migrated. All these indications, indirect though they are, suggest that Neolithic society was much more competent and technologically far more advanced than that of the Mesolithic folk.

The burial practices of the Neolithic peasant farmers, at least for those members of society deemed to merit elaborate burial, involved lengthy and complex ceremonies and the erection of massive monuments. In southern and eastern Britain the bodies were first placed in roofed 'mortuary huts' or fenced 'mortuary enclosures' and allowed to accumulate until a tomb was built to receive them, either on the same site or nearby. The remains placed in the tombs would thus have included both earlier, incomplete and disturbed skeletons and the more recent, still articulated corpses of many individuals, perhaps up to fifty or more but often far fewer, of both sexes and all ages. The tombs themselves, the 'earthen long barrows' (46 *et seq.*), are great mounds, usually between about thirty and fifty yards in length and perhaps a dozen or so feet high, rectangular or wedge-shaped in plan and thrown up from flanking ditches. Many, if not all, had structural timber features, including retaining palisades and impressive façades or roofed buildings at the broader, usually eastern, end where the burials lay.

If the great scale of these barrows and the enormous quantities of earth and timber used in them imply the expenditure of a great amount of labour and time, the megalithic tombs of the highland west and north are even more spectacular. They were constructed of large and sometimes immense blocks of stone, drystone walling or a combination of both, and covered by mounds and cairns no less massive than those of the earthen long barrows. The earliest may date from the late fourth millennium, and they continued to be erected well into the second, but it will be convenient to describe them together. Two broad categories have been defined, in addition to many smaller groups of diverse origins, and local chronological series developing towards either more elaborate or more degenerate forms. The first category, the 'gallery graves' (51-56, 59, 70-72), with concentrations round the Severn estuary and in the Solway–Clyde area, consists basically of a long chamber or gallery, sometimes partitioned off into segments or opening on to additional compartments at its sides and end, approached from a hollow forecourt at the end of a long mound. The second class, the 'passage graves' (62-67), have a main chamber set deep inside a circular cairn and approached by a long passage; here, too, the main chamber may have additional alcoves opening from it. Many megalithic tombs have been robbed or denuded of their stones and covering mounds, leaving only the chamber, while elsewhere some may perhaps never have been enmounded; there are many such free-standing tombs, 'dolmens' or 'cromlechs' (60, 61), whose original appearance and classification are difficult to establish.

Although the megalithic tombs differ in many respects from the earthen long barrows, there are some features shared by both. The burials, for example, are generally inhumations and multiple, but since it was possible to reopen the chambers of megalithic graves, repeated interments took place over long periods, in some cases as long as a thousand years, incidentally showing scant regard for any earlier burials, which were removed or unceremoniously pushed aside. Like the earthen barrows, they also conceal other internal structures besides the burial chambers, and there is abundant evidence for the ritual activities that attended the deposition of burials and the construction of the tomb.

Two other kinds of religious activity deserve mention. One is the practice, within the passage grave tradition and occasionally in other contexts as well, of decoration in the form of abstract motifs, some of which may be traced back to anthropomorphic representations of a 'Mother Goddess', while others had become little more than good-luck or fertility symbols (73-77). Such markings are most magnificently represented in the passage graves of Ireland, but some of the stones in British tombs carry related decoration. The other manifestation of fertility concepts consists of the small figurines of obese females, carved phalli and stone balls, which have been found in every type of Neolithic monument—graves, camps, flint mines and (at a later date) temples (36-38).

The massive scale, complexity and precision in planning and construction of megalithic and earthen tombs, the size and supposed functions of the causewayed camps and the very practice of farming itself, all indicate some degree of social cohesion among the earlier Neolithic communities. For certain purposes at least they came together into sizeable units, within which there could have arisen some form of established administrative organization and social institutions, although this need not imply the stratification of society into distinct classes. But differentiation existed, if only between those individuals or families entitled to tomb burial and those not (the occurrence of both sexes and children and young persons as well as adults suggests that this was a family prerogative), and the great importance clearly attaching to ceremonial burial may imply some kind of religious leadership. The indications, however indistinct, suggest that Neolithic society was becoming both complex and organized, involving a great amount of co-operative activity by many individual settlement groups.

Later Neolithic 2100-1650 BC

Towards the end of the third millennium and the beginning of the second, Britain was subjected to a series of numerous, but individually small-scale, immigrations of people belonging to two highly distinctive new traditions. They found an existing population in which the Insular element was by now expanding and had indeed almost overwhelmed or completely fused with the farming communities into something like a uniform culture throughout most of Britain, but with a certain regional diversity, especially in the north.

The first of the two new elements, the 'Rinyo-Clacton culture', was of an uncertain but probably western French origin. It has a wide but discontinuous distribution in the east, south and extreme north, where it is best represented in the Orkneys, and is characterized by new pottery styles, distinctive burial and ritual monuments and new types of equipment that should be clearly distinguished from those of the contemporary Insular folk (80, 81, 84-6). The other important intrusive element, ultimately of Iberian origin and forming part of the complex movements of communities throughout Europe at this time, is known collectively as the 'Beaker cultures' (87 *et seq.*). In Britain it embraces a wide diversity of groups immigrating over a period of centuries from different homelands and subsequently producing, by local development and varying contacts with existing communities, a series of characteristically British forms. Some of the Beaker folk can be seen to have originated in the Rhineland, others in the Low Countries, and yet others from further west, in France. Britain thus presents a highly complex picture of isolation, interaction and amalgamation of these three elements, within which it is impossible to trace any uniform pattern throughout the country.

It is in their burial and religious practices that the clearest archaeological distinctions lie between the two new cultures and the existing Neolithic peoples. The dead of the Rinyo-Clacton folk were cremated, not inhumed, and buried individually, not collectively, in small pits under flat ground, rarely accompanied by more than the bone pin that secured the now-vanished container for the bones. Such graves might be grouped together into cemeteries (109), associated in many cases with the ritual 'henge' monuments discussed below. The graves of the Beaker tradition were also single, but by inhumation, and characteristically furnished with the personal possessions of the dead person and a drinking cup, possibly made specially for the purpose (87-91, 98-105). The body was carefully placed with the legs slightly flexed or tightly drawn up and perhaps trussed in a variety of containers—of wicker, wood or stone slabs—or in a simple pit (93, 95-97). Some of the burials lie under round barrows, while others, more especially in Scotland and the extreme north of England, are under flat ground. The contrast between these two intrusive traditions and the earthen long barrow and megalithic rites could hardly be more complete, yet on occasion the Beaker folk did not shrink from placing their dead in megalithic tombs.

The ritual temples, or 'henges', of the Rinyo-Clacton and Beaker cultures are apparently peculiar to Britain. They consist of one or more oval or circular ditches with internal or external bank, ranging in diameter from a few yards to a quarter of a mile. The Rinyo-Clacton ones (109, 110, 119) normally had a single entrance, and might enclose one or more rings of ritual pits or timber posts, possibly supporting a roofed structure, while elsewhere cremation grave-pits were dug into the interior area or the sides of the ditch. The Beaker henges, on the other hand, usually had two or more entrances and a ring of stones might surround the internal, sacred space (111-114). It is interesting that, despite their differences, these two otherwise distinct cultural groups should share so remarkable a tradition; we cannot say which class of henge was earlier, but they must all be interrelated, another warning against too sharp a division between the various elements in Britain. Other types of ritual monument dating from the same period are the alignments and avenues of free-standing upright stones (115, 117) or of ditch-and-bank earthworks, while the so-called 'cursuses' (118, 119), whose parallel ditches and banks strode across the countryside for up to six miles in extreme instances, may be even earlier, associated with long barrows and mortuary enclosures. The first stone circles and stone alignments of highland Britain (116, 117), sometimes associated with one another or with burials, may also have been built during this same phase.

A characteristic feature of the Neolithic and Bronze Ages is the concentration in certain areas of settlements, burials and temples. The Avebury district (113-115) in north Wiltshire thus contains one of the two largest Beaker henges enclosing a massive stone circle within which are two smaller stone rings, a great processional way marked by two parallel lines of stones and leading to a complex, smaller henge some one and a half miles away, several earthen long barrows and megalithic tombs, the causewayed camp of Windmill Hill, and clusters of Beaker and Bronze Age barrows including the monstrous mound of Silbury Hill (135). The Stonehenge temple (119-122) began as a very modest Rinyo-Clacton henge with a ring of ritual pits, some later used for cremated burials, and altogether no larger than one of the minor stone circles dwarfed by the Avebury henge circle. Later it was the site of elaborate stone structures of the Beaker and Wessex Bronze Age folk, and its immediate area contains a ditched avenue, a great cursus, a causewayed camp, several long barrows and, stretching to the skyline and beyond in all directions, numerous cemeteries of round barrows of all kinds. Concentrations such as these and other lesser ones being revealed by aerial photography as on the gravels of the Upper Thames (118) must represent the nuclei of settlement and trade, and the religious foci of communities spread much further afield.

The economy and daily life of the later Neolithic peoples is but poorly reflected in the archaeological material. In the warmer drier climatic phase that was now beginning and was to last throughout most of the Bronze Age they continued to cultivate cereals, now with barley the staple grain instead of wheat, but on a smaller scale than before. Instead, they were more dependent on animal husbandry, and a tendency towards migrant pastoralism may account for our almost total ignorance of settlement sites, for the widespread connections implicit in the concentration of monuments just mentioned and for the prospecting and trade activities to be discussed below. Apart from the oblique evidence of one or two mortuary huts probably of this period (94), nothing is known of Beaker or Rinyo-Clacton dwellings with the outstanding exception of the villages of Rinyo itself and Skara Brae in the Northern Isles (82, 83). There, the translation of timber structures into durable stone and their chance survival have preserved a vivid record of living conditions. Although the clustering together of several households into a village group is a strictly local feature due to the rigour of the climate, we may perhaps recreate in our imagination the equivalent houses with their elaborate and sophisticated internal furnishings—beds, dressers and containers—made of timber and other perishable materials in the rest of Britain.

The mutual relationships of the indigenous and immigrant cultural groups are extremely difficult to establish. Their distinctive characteristics reflect divisions between community and community, individual and individual, but only for as long as each stood in isolation from the rest in any particular area. There is no *a priori* reason why cultural diversity should necessarily involve physical conflict, nor need any one element have become established as a superior society or class. The 'weapons' found in Beaker graves could simply represent hunting equipment, the symbols of hunting prowess or an age-group or some other division within a peaceful and unstratified society. On the other hand, the kind of migrant pastoralism that appears to have been practised could give rise to warfare based on cattle raiding and to social divisions such as are known in other 'heroic' societies. In one respect the Beaker folk did play a prominent role—the introduction of the earliest metal objects to Britain and the pioneering, perhaps together with some of the later passage grave builders, of the first metal industry in Ireland and Britain.

Although only the very smallest minority of Beaker graves yield metal goods (98-100, 103, 105) many of which may have been brought from their continental homelands or belong to a late phase of colonization, after native metalworkers had become established, it must have been Beaker prospectors who sought out the copper and gold ores of highland Britain and prepared the way for, if they were not themselves, the craftsmen who introduced the knowledge of metal extraction, smelting and casting. For this reason, if no other, the Beaker folk may well have enjoyed a superior status in the eyes of their contemporaries.

Earlier Bronze Age 1650-1200 BC

It is the metal industries that provide most of our information about British prehistory during the middle centuries of the second millennium BC. Apart from graves with their furnishings, a few hoards and numerous stray finds, there is little other evidence to illustrate economic and daily life. Stock-breeding remained the basis of the subsistence economy as in the later Neolithic, and rising prosperity and a steadily increasing population lie behind the encroachment of settlers into previously unoccupied territory, significantly just those areas of western and northern Britain best suited to pastoral activities. Only in Cornwall is there any indication of a more settled type of arable farming, but we cannot judge the extent of this economy. The introduction of metal equipment had little effect at first on everyday life; axes would be barely as efficient as ground flint and stone ones, let alone superior to them, so long as they were made of copper, and it was only when a knowledge of alloying made it possible to manufacture articles of bronze that metal tools became functionally effective, and even so their cost would put them beyond the means of most of the population.

The first metal axes would have greater ritual significance than serviceability, and there is abundant evidence that the axe—the essential tool of the farmer—possessed symbolic meaning; we thus find specimens made from materials such as chalk, others obviously unused in fine stone like jade, votive hoards of broken axes and carvings and amulets imitating their shape (125-30). Many other items are authority or status symbols, or personal ornaments and costume jewellery, while small knives and bodkins would be the sewing equipment of wealthy ladies. Meanwhile the most important advantages of metal lay in the manufacture of military weapons: long, stout blades hilted as daggers and later elongated into dirks and rapiers, or mounted at the tip of a shaft as spearheads or at right-angles to the handle as 'halberds' (140-2, 145, 151-152).

The rise of prominent individuals, families or classes and the warfare implicit in the manufacture of weapons should be linked with the growth of trade. The main thorough-fares linking Europe with the rich gold and copper desposits of Ireland and Wales and the tin, copper and gold of Cornwall ran through Wessex, and it was there that a highly organized pressure group arose, dominating the trade routes and controlling the passage of goods, as was happening elsewhere at the same time in Europe. Not only wealth but also political power came to be vested in the ruling class in Wessex, and the graves demonstrate a clear division between lavishly furnished burials of chieftains and their ladies, rich but less spectacular ones of a warrior caste, and quite poor ones of the ordinary folk. The ladies wore necklaces of amber from Jutland, blue-glazed 'faience' beads from Egypt and buttons covered with Irish gold (146-8); their lords had ornamented staffs of office, daggers with gold-studded pommels and costume pins from central Europe (140-5), and all lay beneath the elaborate round barrows of distinctive local forms and sometimes enormous size (134-9). From the Mediterranean civilizations, most especially Mycenean Greece (149, 150), to Ireland, from Spain to Scandinavia, the trade routes carried not only metal goods and trinkets but also the secrets of metallurgical techniques and doubtless many other ideas.

Outside Wessex, rich graves containing similar furnishings bear witness to the control exerted by these chieftains over much of southern England and reaching East Anglia. Meanwhile northern Britain, with its own metal resources and local industry, shows comparable but less spectacular burials; the trade routes from Ireland and Scotland to Scandinavia passing north of Wessex doubtless fed this culture, which provided southern England with its own particular material for personal ornaments, Yorkshire jet (153, 154). At the same time, Cornwall held a position of great economic importance because of its tin supplies, one of the very few sources in Europe of this essential element in the bronze alloy; it avoided direct political domination from Wessex and its distinctive pottery styles suggest a local immigration during the fifteenth century BC, to which the intensive plough agriculture mentioned earlier may also be attributed.

Apart from this colonization of Cornwall and the possibly north German origin of the

Wessex chieftains, the pottery and burial rites (162-70) of the period represent a wholly insular development from existing cultures. Where Beaker traditions predominated, the graves were identical with Beaker ones except that the drinking cups were replaced by 'food vessels' of several types, each combining Beaker with Insular Neolithic features (158, 159). Elsewhere, fusion along different lines led to the 'collared' or 'overhanging rim' urns which normally accompanied cremations—themselves a Rinyo-Clacton rite (160, 161). The practice of cremation began to supersede the Beaker-originated rite of individual inhumation during the sixteenth century BC in both Wessex and the north, and by the end of the period was universal throughout Britain. By the same time, too, there had arisen a wide variety in the forms of cremation urns (168, 169), matched by a great diversity in the cremation rites themselves. It is impossible to tell, in the absence of grave goods, whether these different urns and ritual practices represent different periods, cultures or classes or merely private preference. But if the pottery record is reliable, the heterogeneous cultural elements that were still distinct at the beginning of this period—Insular Neolithic, Rinyo-Clacton, Beaker, Wessex and Cornish—had, by its end, become fused into a single undifferentiated entity with a specifically British character.

The outstanding religious monument of the earlier Bronze Age is Stonehenge (119-122). After the early, small temple of the Rinyo-Clacton folk, the Beaker peoples planned a double circle of 'bluestone' (a special kind of igneous rock) uprights with an elaborate entrance, but never completed it, although the stones were laboriously transported from the Presely hills of Pembrokeshire (123). Finally, under the Wessex chieftains, the existing great circle with continuous lintel architrave and the internal horseshoe setting of five trilithons (pairs of uprights with a horizontal capstone) were erected of massive blocks of sarsen, a type of sandstone from north Wiltshire (124), and the bluestones dressed and re-used to form a smaller circle and horseshoe, each within its sarsen counterpart. The labour, time and manpower involved in all these operations, the meticulous planning and superb masonry work, and the complex organization behind the whole enterprise, all indicate the compelling religious fervour of the people, the far-reaching authority of their leaders and the supreme sanctity of the site.

As to the nature of the religious concepts enshrined in the Stonehenge structures, we can only guess. Their orientation, like that of other ritual sites elsewhere, is roughly related to the midsummer sunrise and midwinter sunset, but this may imply nothing more precise than ceremonies associated with the seasons of the agricultural year. However, there are other indications of some kind of sun cult in such articles as the small gold plates with cruciform decoration and the gold-bound amber discs from Wessex graves (150) and the gold-inlaid, boat-shaped bowl from Caergwrle in Flintshire (156), all of which may have affinities with the sun symbolism of Scandinavia. Another cult, that of the axe, has already been mentioned; although already ancient in Britain, the carvings of axes on the Stonehenge sarsens and stone slabs in contemporary cist burials suggest a fresh stimulus, perhaps from Mediterranean axe cults (128-30). Finally, such enigmatic motifs as the feet and other symbols in rock carvings may be a late version of passage grave art (131, 132), and the widespread 'cup-and-ring' markings may belong to the secret mysteries of the metalworkers both here and in other countries (133).

The communities who carried on the native metal industry in Ireland and highland Britain were set apart by their craft from the rest of society. They would form a kind of secret guild, part of a great international organization through which were transmitted the improved techniques of extraction and casting that can be traced throughout the Bronze Age. The procedures involved in bronze metallurgy included prospecting and recognition of the characteristic ores of copper (probably the oxide ores found on or near the surface) and, in quite separate and rare regions, the distinctive deposits of tin; the smelting of the ores in a closed furnace at great heat under a forced draught, in order to reduce them to actual metal; the melting of the metals in crucibles and their alloying in the required proportions; and finally the casting of the molten metal in stone or clay moulds of increasing complexity to produce hollow and elaborately shaped objects. All these procedures would demand not only long training but also a wide practical scientific knowledge of chemistry, physics and geology. The relations of such skilled craftsmen with the rest of society, and in particular with the wealthy classes who were their customers and possibly their masters, remain unknown. But in prehistoric as in all later times the main incentive to technological advance and industrial growth was provided by the military demands of the powerful pressure groups, struggling to maintain and extend their influence, with their constant insistence on more effective weapons and ever greater mass-production.

The growth of Early Britain

Later Bronze Age 1200-500 BC and later

The last centuries of the second millennium saw the beginning of a long series of changes and folk migrations that were to continue and intensify until the Roman Occupation and cumulatively to transform the whole British scene. Unfortunately, by the accident of archaeological survival, the kinds of material at our disposal differ too widely from area to area and period to period for individual migrations to be identified or continuous patterns followed, especially across the boundary between bronze-using and iron-using cultures.

The first innovation that we can detect was the introduction in the twelfth century BC of new types of metal goods of northern and central European origin (171-175), and the rise of a local metal industry in southern Britain, breaking the monopoly of the Irish-Highland centres. At about the same time there is the first evidence of a widespread, intensive agricultural economy and progressive methods of animal husbandry in southern England. These two phenomena may perhaps not be related, but the new metal types could represent not an internal development within the bronze industry, but actual colonization, and the farming changes may imply the immigration of communities or family groups, even though these may at first have been few in number.

The pottery is singularly unhelpful as an indicator of cultural conditions. The coarse, simple 'bucket urns' (182) give little indication of regional or chronological divisions and are so undifferentiated, like their continental counterparts, that they cannot be used as evidence for or against a foreign origin. The 'barrel urns', with a more restricted distribution, display Rinyo-Clacton elements and have no features that need imply a foreign origin, but the third class of pottery, the 'globular urns' (183), is distinctive and novel; even if no satisfactory ancestry has yet been discovered, both they and a few single vessels from settlement sites (184) suggest affinities with northern France. The burial rites can equally well be derived from existing native traditions, and the growing practice of cemetery burial—the characteristic continental rite—has adequate native precedents. In northern and western Britain no detectable change can be seen between this and the preceding period except in the metal industries; whatever external factors affected the south, their influence seems to have been restricted to that area.

At about the turn of the second-first millennium, other changes of great economic consequence took place in the metal industry. First, the true slashing sword was introduced and soon became standard equipment throughout Britain (199). Secondly, new techniques in the casting of bronze (207-11) led to a great expansion of output with two main results: bronze was now within the purchasing range of a far wider consumer market, and efficient tools, especially those of the carpenter, became available to rural craftsmen (206). The new methods may have included the discovery and extraction of the sulphide ores of copper which, though more abundant than the surface oxide ores, required deep mining and more complicated methods of preliminary treatment before they could be reduced to actual metal. In casting, too, a more advanced mass-production technique was introduced—the 'lost wax (*cire perdue*) method'. In this, a model of the required object is made of wax or lead in a stone or bronze mould; the model is then entirely enveloped in clay which is fired to a red heat, turning the clay to pottery and causing the model to melt and run out, leaving a cavity into which the molten metal is poured to produce a final casting requiring little further trimming. Various other technical advances, including the use of sheet metal (201-3), followed in the eighth and seventh centuries BC, and at roughly the same time there were further changes in the organization of both the manufacturing and distributive sides of the industry, but none of these, important as they were economically, involved any appreciable migration of peoples outside the industrial community itself.

The farming economy associated with the users of bucket, barrel and globular urns in southern England, the 'Deverel-Rimbury culture', was still mainly confined to the lighter, upland soils of Wessex and Sussex. It involved the intensive and semi-permanent cultivation of enclosed fields and the continuous occupation of the same sites for decades and perhaps generations. Many of the so-called 'Celtic' fields (186) on the slopes of the chalk downlands are of Iron Age or Roman date, but some originated in the later Bronze Age; they are small plots of one to one and a half acres, bounded by banks or terraces, and were worked with a plough. The latter was probably wholly of timber, since no metal plough parts have been identified, but need not for that reason have been ineffective, especially on the chalk and limestone soils; the slight scratch marks that still sometimes survive represent the very tip of the plough share and by no means the whole depth of the furrow (190-1). The staple crop was still barley, but a new variety was introduced into some areas together with the practice of parching the grain to prevent germination or to facilitate threshing; accidental over-heating accounts for the survival of collections of charred grain. The harvest was gathered with short-handled sickles with flint or (possibly) metal blades. Some form of crop rotation may have been evolved in order to restore the soil, or the fields may have been fertilized with collected manure, by turning the flocks and herds on to the fields after harvest or by burning the stubble. Some such practice must have existed if the land was to be cropped repeatedly, and would be one reason why arable farming was always accompanied by stock-breeding.

The livestock, as before, comprised cattle (perhaps including a new breed), sheep, goats and swine, together with the first undoubted tame breed of horse. One significant feature was the rise in the sheep population and a corresponding decrease in swine, owing in part to the gradual deforestation that accompanied the permanent enclosure of fields. Advanced methods of stock-breeding find expression in several different kinds of earth-works. In the fen areas of East Anglia and the West Country, timber trackways were laid down for the movement of livestock from the settlements to pasture, while on the Sussex and Wessex downs field systems and farmsteads are sometimes associated with hollow trackways for the same purpose, together with small cattle enclosures and the boundary ditches of extensive ranch areas. Here stock-breeding and cereal production were complementary elements in a mixed farming economy, but elsewhere, in Devon and Cornwall and possibly also in northern England, the economy was based predominantly or entirely on the flocks and herds. Dartmoor indeed presents an interesting contrast between its eastern, drier slopes containing the isolated farmsteads and field systems of a mixed economy, and the wetter, south- and west-facing slopes on which lie stone-walled 'pounds' up to about four acres in extent, enclosing a few huts and with pens and sheds built up against the perimeter wall—sites specifically designed for stock-breeding communities (185).

The dwellings were circular huts, up to about twenty feet in diameter and built, according to locally available material, with walls of wattle and clay panels in a framework of upright timber posts or of drystone masonry (187-9). Their conical thatched roofs were supported by the walls and sometimes a central post, supplemented in the largest examples by an additional internal ring of timbers. The interior would contain a hearth in most cases, but sometimes this was a communal feature serving a number of dwellings and placed outside the huts. It was not uncommon for a group of up to about a dozen such huts, not necessarily all in use at one time as habitations, to lie within a palisaded or walled enclosure (189). Such a farmstead settlement would be self-sufficient, except for the metal objects purchased from a pedlar or itinerant bronze founder from time to time: perhaps axes, carpentry tools and occasionally a bucket or cauldron of sheet bronze or costume pins. Domestic crafts included pottery-making, the manufacture of any wooden implements and household equipment, and weaving, for we now find clay weights to keep the warp threads taut on the loom and discs to keep the spindle turning while twisting the yarn (193, 194). Woven woollen textiles had been made in the earlier Bronze Age, if not before, but the increase in the numbers of sheep and the appearance of new weaving equipment suggest that this craft had become more important and perhaps imply the introduction of new techniques.

Such a group of huts was neither village nor hamlet, but a homestead housing about a score of individuals, perhaps grandparents, their children and grandchildren. Communities of this size are also implied by the cremation cemeteries of southern England, containing up to one hundred or more graves and sometimes clustering round a primary 'patriarchal' burial. Households might actually have owned their fields as well as their flocks and herds, although the great ranches of several square miles would presumably have been common land. It may be that wealth was heritable, and that this was one reason why graves were unfurnished, and there is some evidence for 'money' in the form of gold and bronze rings and even some of the socketed axes, which suggests a new type of commerce from the earlier barter of goods and produce. Tentative as these economic interpretations are, they show a consistent trend towards a much more carefully regulated economy than ever before.

While the economic effects of a greatly expanded metal production would have been widespread, there is nothing to indicate any accentuation of the class divisions within society. On the contrary, the uniformity of the burials might be taken to imply a classless social structure were it not that purely religious considerations might forbid any differentiation in graves, especially since no grave goods were deposited. Evidence of a class of aristocratic chieftains (176-80, 204, 205) is supported by the specialized metal hoards from towards the end of this period, containing wagon parts and harness fittings such as were used by the ruling classes of contemporary societies on the Continent (212, 214). The abundance of military equipment (199-200), including such costly items as swords, fine spearheads sometimes inlaid with gold and ceremonial shields of thin bronze, pre-supposes a warrior caste, not otherwise known from the peasant settlements; these give little indication of disturbed conditions or warfare, such as must have obtained if the weapon finds have any meaning, and of whose historical nature, causes and effects we know nothing.

Celtic Iron Age 500 BC–AD 43 or later

The iron-using communities of Britain from the sixth century BC onwards present a wholly different picture for purely archaeological reasons. The burial record ceases almost completely, to be replaced by finds from settlement and military sites; the metal hoards disappear because of the fundamentally different organization and techniques of iron smithing (232-4) from those of bronze working; and finally, the pottery and associated metal objects are sufficiently distinctive to define regional groupings, chronological phases and continental origins. But because the sources are so different, it is exceptionally difficult to study the interaction of the immigrant communities with the native population in time and space in the period of transition, and to distinguish the element of continuity that must have been very strong despite the differences in the surviving material finds. Certainly there was no abrupt end to a 'Bronze Age' and beginning of an 'Iron Age'; many intermediate stages, in which the use of iron gradually permeated the existing peoples in different areas and groups of colonists established themselves in greater or smaller numbers, lie behind the latest bronze hoards and the earliest iron-using settlements, and bronze-using cultures survived locally, particularly in the remoter parts of highland Britain, until perhaps the second century BC and even later. The advantages of iron over bronze are that the ores themselves are far more widespread, that it provides a keener, tougher cutting edge (at least when, by accident or design, some quantity of carbon or other element such as phosphorus either from the ore or entering during smelting gives it a degree of hardness), and that, once the ore has been converted into metal, the manufacture of objects is far simpler. The initial process of reducing the ore, however, involves a long series of highly technical and tedious procedures, and would remain in the hands of professional smelters, but finished objects would be made from the ingots of metal that they produced and traded, by individual blacksmiths in each locality or community. All iron wares were *wrought* (hammered), not cast, until long after prehistoric times in Europe, and none of the elaborate, secret and costly casting processes were involved; little beyond a good bellows, a strong arm and practical experience was required by the local blacksmith.

The middle of the first millennium witnessed great folk movements on the Continent, partly because of a climatic deterioration that caused the abandonment of much heavily populated land in central Europe and more especially along the North Sea coasts, and partly due to political and economic pressures from eastern Europe and the rising power of Mediterranean civilizations. Between about 550 and 350 BC there took place the widespread colonization of much of lowland England by groups of immigrants from the Low Countries and France. These peasant Celtic communities, doubtless quickly amalgamating with the local farming societies, many of whom might be ancestrally related to them, form our Iron Age A cultures (236, 237). They continued to arrive in Britain well into the fourth and third centuries BC, side by side with other bands from continental areas where the La Tène I and II cultures were established—our Iron Age B (238, 239). Some of these came from the Marnian area of north-east France into the south and east of Britain, but are best represented in the rich graves in Yorkshire and eastern England containing war chariots and horse harness; others from Brittany colonized the southwest. Their incursions continued sporadically well into the last century BC in areas peripheral to the Belgic territories of south and south-east England, and indeed both A and B cultures persisted, beyond the limits of Roman control, throughout the first few centuries AD. The Iron Age B immigrations have a distinctly militaristic appearance, and resistance to their invasions is clearly demonstrated by the construction, especially in the third century, of massive defensive structures crowning the hill-tops of southern Britain. Where they combined with the local communities to form what are termed 'AB cultures', the B elements may represent a dominating, military class, which effected the formation of large, closely-knit tribal units for defensive strength, first against the invaders, then against neighbours and finally against the Belgic and Roman armies.

The economy of the Iron Age A peoples was based on mixed farming (the 'Little Woodbury economy', named from a farmstead site near Salisbury) with cereal production as its main element, especially on the downland soils on which the later Bronze Age farmers had flourished. The cereals included oats and a new and hardier variety of wheat, better suited to the wetter climate, although barley remained the staple crop in some parts. Arable cultivation was doubtless greatly helped by the use of metal parts for the plough, in particular the iron share tip and perhaps even a coulter, and harvesting by the availability of iron-bladed sickles (227, 228). Otherwise little change is apparent in agriculture beyond a general indication of greater productivity and prosperity. The farmsteads were basically similar to those of the Bronze Age, but a large circular house surrounded by farm structures, including the characteristic great storage pits (224), now took the place of several separate small huts. These houses (216-19), with concentric rings of stout uprights forming the frames for walls, either of solid timber construction or wattle and clay panels, and supporting a roof of thatch or turf, were later enclosed by a protective palisade and ditch. They indicate prosperous, possibly upper-class, households which may have been the centres of rural estates. More modest, isolated farms would be the standard farming unit throughout the countryside, sometimes tied to the great houses and elsewhere forming independent small-holdings, but none of these have yet been discovered.

The agricultural communities maintained flocks and herds, partly for their dairy produce, meat, leather and other raw materials but also for the manure that was needed to fertilize the fields. There is stronger evidence now for not only some kind of crop rotation but also the application of a dressing of chalk to keep the soil in good heart. Meanwhile, advances can be seen in animal husbandry, especially in the provision of fodder to maintain the food animals through the winters, instead of merely ensuring their survival. The abundance of leaf-knives and billhooks suggests that leaves provided much of the winter feed, supplemented in some areas by the haulms of beans. On the moorlands in and bordering the highland regions of Britain, and chiefly associated with the Iron Age B cultures, stock-breeding formed the main basis of the 'Stanwick economy' so called after the enormous defended area in Yorkshire where the pastoral tribes of northern England assembled with their vast flocks and herds in defiance of Rome in the later first century AD. As before, local conditions determined the proportions of the different animals: sometimes sheep represented almost the entire livestock population, elsewhere horse-breeding would have been predominant, and elsewhere again local forest cover would have favoured swine-herding, but overall the main component of the herds would have been cattle. In certain regions, notably the West Country and south

Wales, great stockaded enclosures with widely spaced ramparts and ditches were constructed on hill-slopes close to a good water supply and good grazing land (281). In Wessex and Sussex, similar but single-banked enclosures have been found underlying or within the great hill forts, which themselves owe at least their size to the need to enclose and protect the flocks and herds of the local farming population.

The large numbers of weapons and other military equipment, including chariots, swords, daggers, spears, lances and slingstones for offence, and shields and helmets for protection, witness to the widespread petty warfare and brigandage of Celtic Britain, but their chief memorial consists in the massive defensive fortresses that are still so prominent a feature of our southern countryside (277-86). These differ so greatly in the scale and plan of their earthworks and the degree of permanence and extent of the settlements within them that no single function or universal interpretation can apply to them all. Some were unoccupied save when imminent danger threatened and the local population sought shelter for themselves and their livestock. Others would house a small permanent garrison, or perhaps the family and retainers of the local chieftain, while yet others show extensive signs of permanent occupation over long periods and even of industrial activities. These last, which include some of the largest of all the hill forts, would thus be almost small townships, providing safe shelter for travelling merchants and country markets, and serving as the administrative centres of the rulers of the local tribal areas.

Impressive as many of these forts are today after the silting of the ditches, the collapse of the ramparts and the disappearance of their timber and stone superstructures, they would have been even more dominating in their original state. The massive artificial defences would make them almost impregnable except by siege, and there is little evidence that any fell except to the Roman or Belgic armies (290). The entrances, which were their weakest point, were often protected by intricate outer earthworks or so designed that attackers would be forced to expose their flanks to defenders manning the ramparts, and the multiplication of ditches may partly be linked with the introduction of sling warfare or merely be the obvious method of strengthening the defences in general and keeping the enemy at greater range. Outside the hill-fort areas, other kinds of defensive structures were erected, especially the cliff castles of south-west Britain and the brochs (287-9) and allied strongholds of the Scottish highlands and islands, which represent heavily protected single farmsteads rather than communal places of refuge.

In economic terms the construction of such elaborate defensive sites, involving enormous quantities of timber, stone and earth and a large expenditure of time and labour, reflects a far greater prosperity and productivity than had previously existed. One of the main factors responsible for this was the use of iron, which brought metal equipment, especially cutting tools and weapons, within the purchasing range of almost every class. The carpenter, wheelwright and wainwright benefited in particular from the wide range of fully efficient tools (230, 231, 243, 244), and the standards of workmanship in these crafts rose to great heights. The increased demand for goods of all kinds resulted in the growth of specialist industries, which would be stimulated by the introduction of such mechanical devices as the lathe. Internal trade flourished and some goods and materials were even exported to the Continent; the famous list given by Strabo in the early first century AD includes corn, livestock, metals, leather, slaves (291) and hunting dogs.

The aristocratic patronage of schools of artist-craftsmen working primarily in bronze and gold but also in humbler materials, is shown by the flowering of a brilliant Insular decorative art, an offshoot from similar styles on the Continent (242, 246, 247, 248 *et seq.*). Its motifs are highly sophisticated, abstract designs, based primarily on the spiral and open circle, and at its best it shows a lively interplay of light and shade, asymmetry and balance, delicate line and swelling plastic shapes, sometimes enhanced (or spoilt) by coral or multi-coloured enamel inlay. One of its most attractive features is the skilful expression of the rare human and animal figures. Many of the fine objects thus adorned would be the favourite possessions of their owners—martial parade equipment (251-64), chariot and harness fittings (245-7), personal jewellery (265-74), toilet articles and drinking vessels (242, 248), as well as the ceremonial insignia of rank or religious office. We can thus gain an insight into the nature of contemporary society and the habits and favourite activities of its leaders—warfare, horsemanship, personal display and feasting.

Of Celtic religions (225, 226) and cults we have little direct evidence in Britain. Anthropomorphic deities (311, 312, 316) symbolize various facets of the natural world and form part of the Celtic pantheon known from later literature. Other wooden figures (317-20) belong to a long line of idols which Christian missionaries were still to encounter many centuries later, and the small animal figures, especially of boars (313-5), horses (307-10) and oxen (303, 306), are part of an equally persistent tradition of animal cults. Even the geometric motifs of Celtic art may ultimately be of a symbolic nature. Votive hoards from former lakes and rivers, which provide much of our decorated metalwork, may reflect the rites in sacred groves associated with the Druids, the Iron Age priesthood whose supra-tribal authority in secular matters and law-giving as well as religion made them so important a nucleus of Celtic nationalism that their suppression was one of Rome's first objectives after the conquest.

Belgic Iron Age 125 BC–AD 43 or later

During the last 150 years of the Celtic Iron Age, parts of southern England were subjected to a quite distinct series of immigrations resulting from Germanic pressure in Belgic Gaul and the Gallic campaigns of Julius Caesar. A first wave of settlers into the lower Thames area soon after 150 BC heralded the beginning of this movement, which led to the foundation of the 'Belgic' or Iron Age C cultures. This first wave is represented only by a series of gold coins, and we cannot assess its meaning in terms of social units. It was followed by others (292) on a larger scale which, from about 100 BC, are accompanied by the burials and material culture of apparently considerable communities, the nucleus of the Catuvellaunian tribal confederacy whose control first extended over Kent and southern Essex and soon afterwards embraced most of the Home Counties, the south Midlands and parts of East Anglia. Later again, at about the time of Caesar's abortive invasions of Britain in 55 and 54 BC, a refugee movement from across the Channel established a second Belgic dynasty, the Atrebates, in central southern England, first in Sussex, Hampshire and Berkshire and subsequently expanding westwards as far as Dorset and Somerset.

The Belgic immigrations and Caesar's invasions bring southern Britain within the range of documented history, illuminated by contemporary written records and inscriptions on coins (293-5). For the first time we can identify tribal groups, individuals and places by name, learn of historical events and trace the dynastic struggles for power between the various members of the ruling families. These need not concern us here, but we should note especially the growing predominance of the Catuvellauni among the Belgic princedoms and the expansion of their power, variously by military, political and diplomatic means, over their neighbours. They thus won the port of Colchester from the Trinovantes of Essex, a prize of the greatest economic importance, and made special efforts to gain control of the iron-producing regions of the Weald from the Cantii of Kent, of the east Midlands from the Coritani and, moving westwards to the Bristol Channel, the rich resources of the Forest of Dean from the Dobunni. The development of commercial and diplomatic relations between Britain and Rome before the Claudian occupation is illustrated partly by Roman historical sources but even more vividly by the arrival and, from about AD 10, the abundance of imported pottery, metalware and trinkets from Italy and occupied Gaul, and their local imitation in Britain. The same trend is also shown by the introduction of silver and bronze denominations into the British coinage, and their copying of Roman 'types' (294), and even by occasional finds of Roman coins themselves in the early first century AD.

Meanwhile an outstanding characteristic of the Belgic cultures was the foundation of urban settlements. These were the administrative centres, coin mints and political capitals of the tribal rulers, admirably sited as markets and set at the junctions of trade and communication routes by sea, river and land. Besides the houses of chiefs and their followers and the huts of craftsmen and traders, they also enclosed shops and workshops and doubtless public buildings, temples and places of amusement. Indeed, except for architectural finesse and graceful living, they fulfilled all the functions of a town in the modern sense, and often occupied the very sites of Roman and later foundations. Although they had their own defensive systems of dykes and earthworks, they differed fundamentally from the Celtic hill forts and represent a major innovation in the settlement pattern of prehistoric England.

The economic basis of the commercial wealth of Belgic Britain must lie in the exports listed by Strabo, and in particular in cereal production. The demands of the towns with their industrial and trading classes would stimulate food production, and Caesar's legions seem to have had little difficulty in victualling themselves from the countryside. Few farmstead sites have been discovered, but some of these lie, significantly, beneath Roman villas—the farms of a highly intensive agricultural economy. The lack of farm sites and their fields is presumably due to the almost continuous cultivation ever since of the medium soils on which they would have been situated, and this in itself is an indication that Belgic farmers—and possibly Celtic ones, too, in non-Belgic areas—were working the more fertile lands as well as upland light soils. The present distribution of Celtic fields need not by any means represent the whole extent of early arable cultivation. There is equally scanty evidence of the scale and nature of animal husbandry on the fine pasture of the Home Counties; it is possible that these areas were used not only for cattle but also for the breeding of horses that by now played a major role in warfare and transport.

As far as crafts are concerned, pottery at least was mass-produced on a truly industrial scale; it was wheel-thrown and fired in specialized kilns which must have involved considerable capital outlay. Its products included traditional burial wares, especially the elegant pedestal urns of the first Belgic cultures, fine table services including cups, platters and beakers, and a wide range of domestic, cooking and storage vessels (296 *et seq.*). Bronze founding was another industry carried on in the urban workshop quarters, and the technique of spinning enabled fine, thin-walled bowls to be produced, while the blacksmith would have a place in both urban and rural settlements, producing wrought ironwork of outstanding merit (306). Other specialist industries may have included weaving, goldwork, enamelling and the lathe turning of vessels and personal ornaments in shale, a form of fossilized wood (297), for the flourishing urban markets and the demands of the ruling castes, and salt panning along the east coast.

The rigid stratification of Belgic society is reflected in a sharp distinction between poorly and richly furnished graves. The finest of these contain brooches, wine-drinking equipment and richly decorated buckets as well as pottery (298–300), but the most spectacular are the 'vault burials' of the Catuvellauni (305). These yield a wealth of native and imported pottery, bronze vessels, wine pitchers and iron hearth fittings, besides more personal possessions, accompanying the cremated bones which were placed in a casket on or near a couch or litter. The picture of the barbarian luxury of Belgic princely life that these provide would be equally applicable to the chieftains of contemporary Celtic societies, whose richest graves contain material (302–4), witnessing to the trade which was carried on between Celtic and Belgic areas.

Belgic society, material equipment, government and commerce and the growth of urban centres were all strongly influenced by the Roman provincial world, and provide a stepping stone from the prehistoric to the Roman period in Britain. After Caesar's failure at occupation, the first Roman emperors judged the control that they already held over Britain by trade and diplomacy to outweigh the major hazards of full-scale overseas military operations. In AD 43, however, military and political conditions impelled Claudius to mount an invasion, and his legions succeeded, not without difficulty, in bringing much of the country under the yoke of Rome, although the Iron Age cultures of the north remained unaffected for centuries. In northernmost Scotland there flourished the builders of the 'broch' farmsteads and great stone houses (220, 221); south of these, from the Forth to the Moray Firth, a different type of fortress may represent the peoples who were later to become the Picts of history (whose name has been applied indiscriminately to sites of many periods and regions); while in the Scottish Lowlands, northern England, Wales and south-west England, varying Roman control and trade made little impact on the native way of life outside the military stations and frontier posts. Even within the urbanized, civil areas of the Roman province, at the end of a dozen and more generations of alien civilization, Celtic culture still retained sufficient vitality to flower anew in the troubled centuries after the Roman withdrawal—eloquent testimony indeed to the strength of the traditional heritage of prehistoric Britain.

1

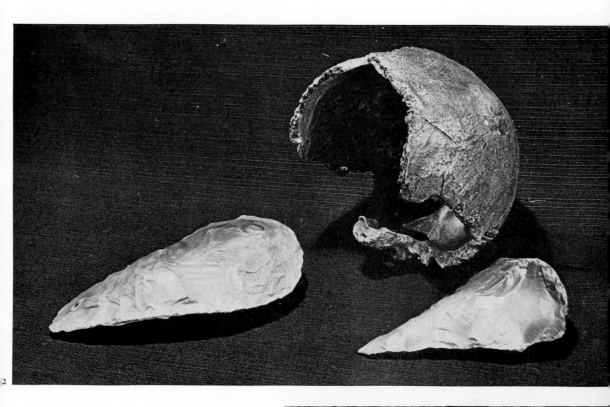

2

3

1 Wooden spear-tip from *Clacton-on-Sea*, *Essex*, the oldest wooden implement. Found with flint scrapers and other tools. 15 in. long. Lower Palaeolithic. 400–300,000 BC. [BM(NH)]

2 Cast of part of a skull from Thames gravels at *Swanscombe*, *Kent*, with hand-axe tools from the same site. The skull, the earliest from Britain, may be of *Homo sapiens* type. 250–200,000 BC [MM]

3 Part of an early Palaeolithic camping site at *Cuxton*, *Kent*, showing 3 hand-axes lying together. The earliest British dwelling site discovered undisturbed. 250–200,000 BC (1 ft scale)

4 The development of chipping technique and improved shapes during a period of perhaps 200,000 years in the Lower Palaeolithic. Lengths about 4-5 in. *Northfleet, Kent.* [CMAE]

5 Hand-axes from the *Thames* gravels, showing the range in size from about 1 ft (a cast) to about 5 in. of these multi-purpose tools. 300,000–200,000 BC. [RM]

6 Flake tools of an advanced kind (Levalloisian) with a carefully prefabricated core about 5 in. long for striking flakes of prepared shape like that in the foreground. 200,000–100,000 BC. [RM]

7

8

7 *Cheddar Gorge, Somerset*. Mouths of natural caves in limestone areas such as this were occupied seasonally by Upper Palaeolithic hunters from about 60,000 BC.

8 *Paviland Cave, Glamorgan*, occupied by Upper Palaeolithic man and containing occupation debris and the earliest deliberate burial of a young man, his bones stained with red ochre. Cave mouth about 30 ft high.

9

10

11

9 Upper Palaeolithic flint borers and scraper from *Gough's Cave, Cheddar*; made from 'blades' and used for preparing leather and wood. Scraper on right $2\frac{1}{2}$ in. long. About 25,000–10,000 BC. [GCM]

10 Upper Palaeolithic flint points, used as insets in composite tools, perhaps wooden-handled knives or weapons. Lengths about $1\frac{1}{2}$-2 in. 25,000–10,000 BC. *Gough's Cave, Cheddar*. [GCM]

11 Finely flaked 'laurel leaf' points showing the excellence of flintworking techniques in Upper Palaeolithic times. Larger point $4\frac{1}{2}$ in. long. *Soldier's Hole, Cheddar*. About 20,000 BC. [GCM]

12

13

14

12 Two antler 'bâtons-de-commandement' (one fragmentary) and an ivory rod, perhaps part of a composite bow. The bâtons may be ceremonial staffs. *Gough's Cave, Cheddar.* Upper Palaeolithic, 15,000–10,000 BC. Length of complete bâton 6½ in. [GCM]

13 Upper Palaeolithic engraving of a horse's head on a rib bone from *Robin Hood's Cave, Creswell Crags, Derbys.* Natural size. 15,000–10,000 BC. [BM]

14 Upper Palaeolithic personal ornaments of pierced teeth and mollusc shell, with a bone borer marked along the edges, perhaps as a tally. Borer 3½ in. long. *Gough's Cave, Cheddar.* 25,000–10,000 BC. [GCM]

15 Engraving of a stylized human figure, possibly a masked male dancer, from *Pin Hole Cave, Creswell Crags.* Human representations are extremely rare in Upper Palaeolithic art. Natural size. 15,000–10,000 BC. [BM]

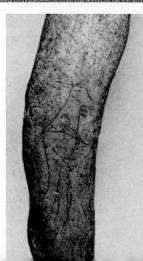

15

16

17

18

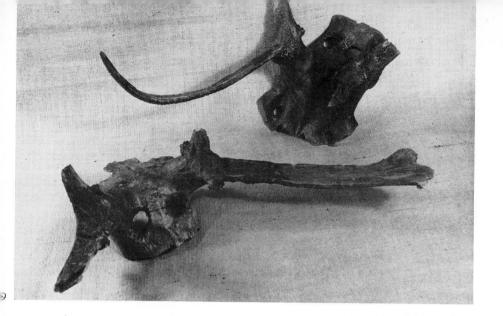

9

20

21

6 Part of the Mesolithic lakeside platform of birch wood at *Star Carr, Seamer, Yorks*, a settlement of forest-dwellers equipped with axes. Eighth millennium BC.

7 A graver, a typical implement of Upper Palaeolithic and Mesolithic times, being used to carve a splinter of antler from which to make a barbed point. *Star Carr, Yorks*. [CMAE]

8 Mesolithic stag antler harpoon heads from *Star Carr, Yorks*; these were mounted as pairs of prongs for fishing, the different types probably for different kinds of fish. Longest just over 13 in. [CMAE]

9 Antler frontlets, the branches hollowed out and the foreheads pierced for wearing on the head, probably in dancing rituals. Antler stub about 10 in. long. Mesolithic. *Star Carr, Yorks*. [CMAE]

10 A selection of Mesolithic flints including scrapers, an axe sharpened by a cross-blow at the tip, and microliths, used as insets in composite tools. Axe about 6 in. long. [BRM]

11 Tools from a Mesolithic site at *McArthur Cave, Oban, Argyll*, including a harpoon for fishing or hunting deer, and bone and stone tools. Harpoon nearly 5 in. long. [NMAS]

22

22 Neolithic causewayed camp at *Windmill Hill, Wilts,* from the air. The three rings of interrupted ditches continued right round to enclose about 20 acres in all

23 A section of the middle ditch at *Windmill Hill* during excavation; an unbroken bank would be built from the ditch material to enclose the cattle. Ditch here about 3 to 4 ft deep

24 Neolithic hut foundation at *Mount Pleasant Farm, Nottage, Glamorgan*. The drystone footings of one wall and inner row of postholes survive from a hut about 8 ft by 18 ft internally, with a ridged roof

23

24

25

26

27

28

25 Pottery of Western Neolithic type, and later, more developed forms. The earliest British pottery, used for storage on an uneven floor or suspended by the lugs, from *Windmill Hill, Wilts.* Tallest nearly 11 in. high. [AM]

26 Pottery of Derivative Neolithic type from a causewayed camp at *Abingdon, Berks.* The heavy rims and lugs and handles are characteristic of this group, the diagonal ornament imitating the sewing of leather vessels on to hoops. Largest 10 in. diam. [AMO]

27 Pottery of a different Derivative Neolithic type from sites in *East Anglia*, with more decoration and the beginnings of hollowed necks. Pot on the right about 1 ft diam. [CMAE]

28 Neolithic pottery from the *Hebrides*, allied both to southern British types and the Rinyo-Clacton forms, but developing local characteristics. Tallest vessel about 1 ft high. [NMAS]

29

29 Flint axes from *Scotland*. These were essential tools for forest clearance farming and timberwork for houses, other structures, tools and domestic utensils. The flint blades were mounted in morticed wooden handles. Lengths from about 4 in. Neolithic. [NMAS]

30 Stone axes from *Scotland*, of specially selected fine-grained rock, ground and polished to a sharp edge,

were the alternative to high-grade flint ones. Lengths about 6 in. Neolithic. [NMAS]

31 Neolithic leather-working equipment from *Windmill Hill*, *Wilts*, the comb for removing rough hair, the gouge for cleaning the pelt and the points for making holes for sewing or used as costume pins. Comb 8 in. long. Neolithic. [AM]

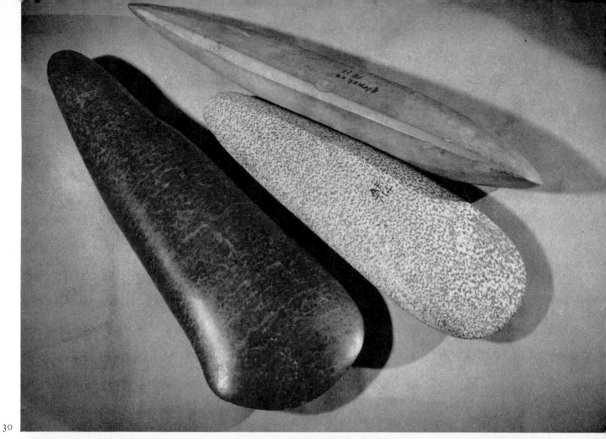

30

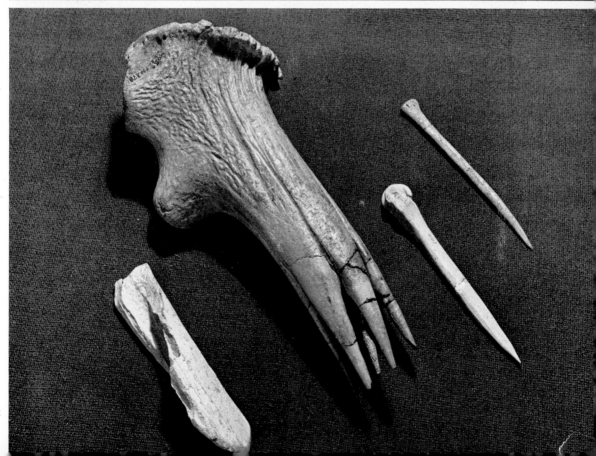

31

32

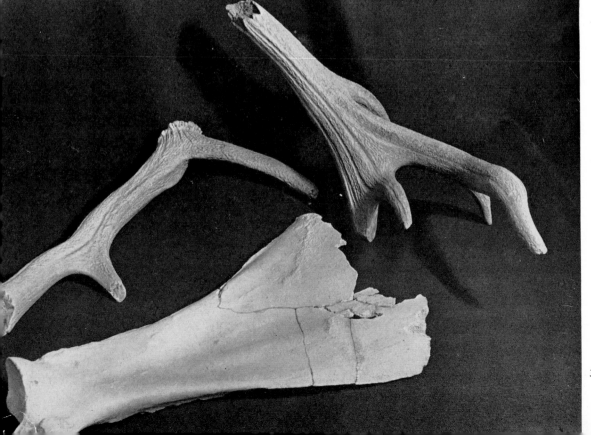

33

34

35

32 Neolithic flint-mine shaft at *Grimes Graves, Norfolk*, showing the radial galleries following the seam of high-quality flint at a depth of up to 30 feet below the surface. The mined flint was roughly shaped into the form of axes and traded throughout much of southern England

33 Flint-mining tools from the *Easton Down* mines, *Wilts*. The chalk blocks were levered out with the antler pick and the rubble collected with antler rakes and shoulder-blade shovels, removed in baskets and hauled to the surface. Similar tools were used in the construction of causewayed camps and burial mounds. Neolithic. Pick about 16 ins. long. [SM]

34 A stone-axe factory site at *Graig Lwyd, Penmaenmawr, Caernarvon*. Roughed-out blocks for axes can be seen in the foreground, and the site is littered with scree, waste flakes, hammerstones and the hearths of the stone workers

35 Products from a stone-axe factory at *Great Langdale, Westmorland*, including waste flakes, a roughed-out axe and a finally ground axe. The flint and stone axe industries are the oldest in Britain. Neolithic. Axe about 5 in. long. [CMAE]

36

36 A Neolithic fertility shrine at *Grimes Graves, Norfolk*, where the flint seam had failed. Behind, an 'altar' of chalk blocks with a female figurine on top and a phallus and chalk balls at the side; in front, a votive offering of flint blocks and the miners' antler picks. The figurine is arrowed

37 The chalk figurine from *Grimes Graves* in the form an obese (pregnant ?) woman; such fertility figur

originate in the Upper Palaeolithic and continue into modern times as harvest 'corn dollies'. Neolithic. $4\frac{1}{2}$ in. high [BM]

38 Chalk-cut fertility figures from *Windmill Hill, Wilts*, including a phallus, a human torso and an incised plaque; comparable figures are known from earthen long barrows and henge monuments. Neolithic. Torso 4 in. tall. [AM]

37

38

39 Engraving of a buck in a remote glen, *Glen Domhain, Argyll*, of unknown but perhaps Mesolithic or Neolithic date and possibly linked with the Arctic cultures. Length about 9 in.

40 Figure of elk or red deer engraved on chalk crust from *Grimes Graves, Norfolk*, possibly reflecting a native Mesolithic tradition among the miners. Length 3 in. [BM]

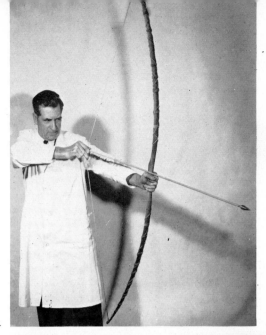

41 Half of a Neolithic long bow of yew from *Meare
Heath, Somerset*, for which a radio-carbon date of
2810–2570 BC has been obtained. Original total length
about 6 ft. [CMAE]

42-3 Details of the *Meare Heath* bow, showing the nock,
half snapped away, and the thin transverse binding
still in position on the limb. Nock 1 in. long; limb
up to nearly 3 in. wide. [CMAE]

44 Reconstruction of the *Meare Heath* bow, showing the
elaborate binding with threads and the diagonal and
transverse leather webbing to strengthen the tips
and limbs [CMAE]

45 Neolithic arrowheads from *Scotland*, with a reconstructed arrow tip showing method of hafting. Such
arrowheads demonstrate the extent of hunting among
Neolithic peoples. Lengths up to about 2 in. [NMAS]

41   43

46 Neolithic earthen long barrow at *Fussell's Lodge,
Wilts*, during excavation. The ditches flank a
wedge-shaped mortuary enclosure of trench-bedded
timbers inside which is a tent-like mortuary hut
covering over 50 burials in bone 'stacks'. Length of
the enclosure 43 yds. A radio-carbon dating of 3410–
3050 BC has been obtained

47 The *Nutbane, Hants* earthen long barrow showing
(extreme top left) the ditch, and elaborate façade

structures, including possibly a roofed building across
the end with massive upright timbers. Behind was a
fenced enclosure containing a ditched mortuary area.
The façade is over 13 yds across. A radio-carbon
dating, possibly of ancient timbers, was 2870–2570 BC

48 The *Nutbane* burials inside the mortuary ditch. All
four are contracted, articulated skeletons, three of
males in their thirties and one, the central, of a 12–13-
year-old child

49 A large Neolithic earthen bank barrow at *Long Bredy, Martin's Down, Dorset*. Overall length over 200 yards; built in two parts, the longer one on two different alignments

50 Mutilated burial of a young man at the end of a bank barrow over one-third of a mile in length at *Maiden Castle, Dorset*. The body had been decapitated, the skull shattered and the limbs amputated. Neolithic

51 *East Kennet, Wilts.* A chambered long barrow of typical, pear-shaped form, 115 yds long, 33 yds wide and about 20 ft high at the eastern end

52 *West Kennet, Wilts.* Air view of the chambered long barrow before excavation; the mound, 110 yds long, is out of all proportion in size to the chamber structures at the east end. A flat berm separates the mound from its flanking ditches, 8 yds wide and 12 ft deep, the northern one being visible in the field in the foreground

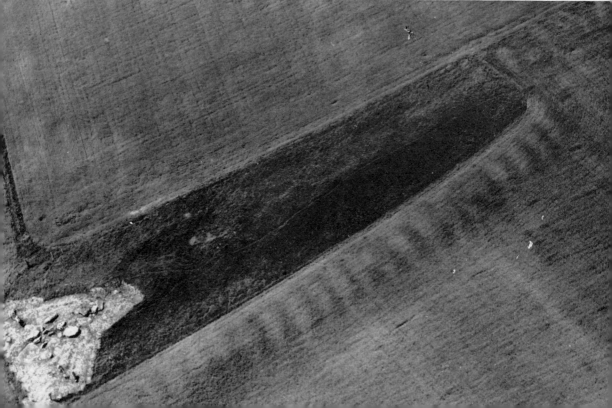

53

54

55

53 Model by R. J. C. Atkinson of the *West Kennet* chambers, showing forecourt lying behind a massive façade. The gallery has two lateral chambers on each side and one at the end. [DM]

54 The *West Kennet* façade, 13 yds across and built of stones ranging from 12 ft in height at the centre to (originally) 7 ft at the outer ends. The three central stones block the small forecourt

55 The *West Kennet* gallery looking inwards; the roof stones leave an 8 ft headroom and gaps between the stones are filled with drystone walling. The whole gallery and chambers were filled with deposits after 1000 years of use of the tomb

56 The burials in the SE chamber at *West Kennet*, showing their disordered and disarticulated condition. Over 46 individuals altogether were represented; in this chamber were only 2 adults, but 9 children and 1 foetus

57

58

57 Long barrow, *Belas Knap, Glos*, from the air. It is 60 yds long and 20 wide at the broad, north end. The chambers do not face the forecourt but are built into the sides and narrow end, and yielded bones of 38 people

58 View of the incurved forecourt at *Belas Knap*, with restored drystone masonry revetment. The lintelled portal with blocking stone is a dummy, backed by the body of the mound, perhaps to mislead evil spirits trying to gain entry to the tomb

59 Megalithic tomb at *Tinkinswood, St Nicholas, Glamorgan*. A long mound with inturned drystone walling forecourt at the east end leading to a rectangular chamber with capstone weighing over 40 tons and containing the remains of at least 50 individuals

60

61

60 *Lligwy dolmen, Anglesey*, from which the cairn
has entirely disappeared. The capstone measures
$18 \times 16 \times 3\frac{1}{2}$ ft and covers a chamber cut out of the
underlying rock to a depth of 6 ft from the roof;
remains of about 30 individuals were found in the
chamber

61 A denuded dolmen of 'Penwith' type, consisting of
a massive capstone, reaching 9 ft in height, covering
a chamber measuring 7 by 9 ft. *Trethevy Quoit,
Cornwall*

62

63

64

62 The entrance to the *Bryn Celli Ddu* passage grave, Anglesey. The kerb of great stone blocks lies in a circular ditch and contains the round cairn of over 30 yds diameter

63 Model of the *Bryn Celli Ddu* passage grave, showing the kerb, small antechambers, passage and central chamber as well as some of the many additional ritual structures. In the foreground is a pit containing the whole skeleton of an ox, flanked by walls and with a timber structure facing the tomb. [NMW]

64 The upright monolith, 6 ft high, in the central chamber at *Bryn Celli Ddu*. The chamber, 8 ft across, is approached by a passage 25 ft long. The monolith may have some phallic meaning; it is carefully rounded and smoothed

65

65 The passage grave of *Maes Howe, Orkney Mainland*. The cairn is separated from an irregular ditch by a wide berm (the wall is modern) and is nearly 40 yds in diameter and 24 ft high

66 The superb architecture of the internal chamber, looking out through the low (4½ ft high) passage of *Maes Howe*. The chamber is 5 yds square with buttressed corners and the stones are finely selected and laid to

form walls that are upright for about 4½ ft and then overlap inwards to form a corbelled roof some 15 ft high

67 A corner of the *Maes Howe* chamber showing a buttressed angle, the beginning of the corbelled roof and one of the three cells opening from the chamber nearly 3 ft from the floor with its blocking stone below

66

67

'Recumbent stone circle' at *Loanhead of Daviot, Aberdeens.* The ring-cairn with open central area has almost entirely disappeared. The stone circle, over 20 yds across, consists of 10 stones, each within a small cairn, and a recumbent stone with flankers. Just outside the circle was a later Bronze Age cemetery

The *Loanhead* recumbent stone, over 11ft long, with its flanking uprights. The symbolism of this feature, found mainly in and around Aberdeenshire, is unknown

The concave forecourt of a gallery grave at *Blasthill, Kintyre,* with the main burial chamber behind the central stones and showing the edge of the long cairn. One of the sw Scottish gallery graves

71 The *Dwarfie Stane, Hoy, Orkney*; a unique rock-cut tomb with a short passage leading into a chamber with side cells. The entrance is 2 ft 10 in. by 2 ft 4 in. and the whole rock slab measures nearly 10 yds in length

72 A 'stalled cairn' at *Midhowe, Rousay, Orkney,* another specialized Scottish type of megalithic tomb. This is the largest of its class, with a chamber 25 yds long divided into 12 compartments and containing 25 burials on slab platforms visible on the left of the photo. The entrance is at the far end and the enclosing rectangular cairn was over 33 yds long and 13 yds wide

73

74

73 One of the rare ornamented stones from British passage graves at *Barclodiad y Gawres, Anglesey*. Possibly a highly stylized 'mother goddess' figure with zig-zag arms and necklace, spiral 'eyes' above, and lozenges for navel and sexual parts. Height 5½ ft

74 Decorated bone plaque, 5 in. long, from *Jarlshof, Shetland Mainland*, in the style of plaque idols of the early metal age in Iberia and also probably the ultimate stylization of a mother goddess figure. Early second millennium BC. [NMAS]

75

76

77

75 Spiral-decorated stone from *Barclodiad y Gawres, Anglesey.* The spirals are here arranged for decorative effect and may symbolize fertility or good luck. The designs are pecked with a stone maul. Width of stone about 4 ft. Neolithic

76 Double-spiral 'eye' motif on a stone from *Calder-stones Park, Liverpool, Lancs,* possibly the remains of a passage grave. The motif recurs in Ireland and Atlantic Europe and later in early metal-working contexts in Britain (*cf* pl. 155). Each spiral about 6 in. diameter. Neolithic

77 Another carving from the *Calderstones, Liverpool,* of a pair of stylized feet (the right about 10 in. long), such as are also found on the Continent, in Scotland and in Scandinavia. Early second millennium

78

79

78 Insular Neolithic pottery from the *Thames*, showing the profuse decoration; the hollow neck is characteristic, possibly developing from Derivative Neolithic styles (pl. 27). Taller pot 7 in. diameter. Late third to early second millennium. [LM]

79 Insular Neolithic pottery with different ornament and showing the development of a very heavy rim (back), leading in the early second millenium to the straight sided, flat based vessel with 'collar' (right). From the *Thames*, possibly votive bowls. Back vessel 6 in. tall [LM]

80

81

80 Rinyo-Clacton equipment from *Woodhenge* and *Durrington Walls, Wilts*. Note the flat bases of the pottery and the flint arrowheads that are typical of this culture. Tall vessel nearly 6 in. high. [SM]

81 Later Neolithic flint equipment, showing the very high standard of knapping: arrowheads, discoidal and 'slug' knives, axe (imitating a metal form) and sickle blade. From the *London area*. Sickle 7 in. long. [LM]

82
83

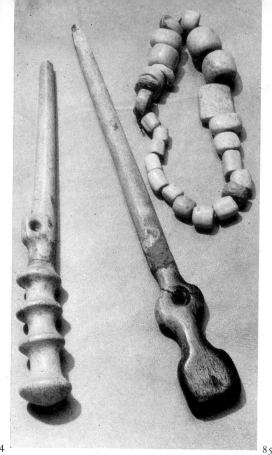

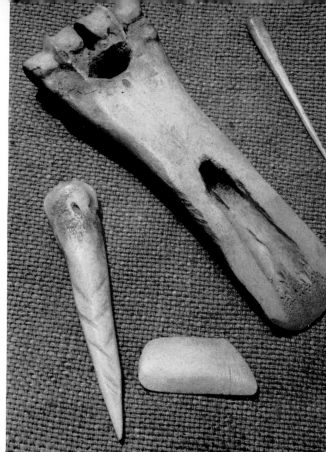

82 The Rinyo-Clacton village of *Skara Brae, Orkney Mainland*. Eight huts huddle together, linked by a maze of covered passages and formerly covered by their own midden. Such village groups occur only in the Northern Isles at this time

83 Interior of hut 7 at *Skara Brae*, measuring about 17 by 16 ft internally and showing flag-bordered beds, the central hearth with stone seat, lined tanks let into the floor, a stone 'dresser' and a corner cell built into the thickness of the wall. The roof would be partly corbelled, closed in the centre with thatched or turfed rafters

84 Bone and ivory ornaments from *Skara Brae*. The pins (longer nearly 10 in.) were used for fixing costume, and have affinities with the Irish passage grave equipment and with Atlantic Europe. Late Neolithic. [NMAS]

85 Heavy bone gouge, bone points and polished flake from *Skara Brae*; the widespread use of bone instead of flint gives a strongly Mesolithic appearance to the equipment from the site. Gouge nearly 8 in. long. Late Neolithic. [NMAS]

86 Carved stone balls, perhaps ceremonial mace heads, found mainly in eastern Scotland and the Northern Isles. Compare the ornament on the bottom one with pl. 155. Diameter 2½–3 in. Probably early second millennium. [NMAS]

87 A fine bell-beaker from the *West Kennet* long barrow *Wilts*, showing unusual decoration with affinities in various parts of the Continent, including Iberia. Height about $7\frac{1}{2}$ in. [DM]

88 Beakers from *Berkshire*. Back: a long-necked form, an Insular development, $7\frac{1}{2}$ in. tall; right: a handled necked beaker; left: a bell-beaker. Note the great variety of decorative techniques and motifs, including vertical panels as well as horizontal zones. [BM]

89 Bell-beaker from a possible habitation site at *Bathgate, West Lothian*, suggesting an origin in the Rhineland or the Low Countries. Beakers were drinking cups, for beer or mead, and would hold between one and two pints. Height nearly 6 in. [NMAS]

90 Handled beakers from *Cambridgeshire*. These are pottery versions of wooden mugs, as is shown partly by the patterns on the bases and partly by the imitation technique of 'chip-carving'. Vessel on the left about 8 in. tall. [CMAE]

90

91

91 Giant pot-beakers and others with rusticated ornament may have been the domestic equivalents of the
fine cups, possibly specially made for burial use.

Rusticated surface treatment survives in East Anglia
throughout the Bronze Age. From *East Anglian
sites*. Giant beaker about 11 in. tall. [CMAE]

92

93

92 A Beaker barrow after excavation, *Normanton, Wilts.*
This double-ditched example yielded no less than 11
burials, mostly of children, interred separately or
sometimes in pairs, perhaps indicating an epidemic

93 A double burial from the entrance gap through the
inner ditch at *Normanton*, containing the remains of
a 9-year-old child and a 1–2-month-old baby accompanied by an ordinary and a tiny beaker

94 A mortuary hut under a round barrow at *Beaulieu,
Hants*, possibly of Beaker date. The walls of small
stakes enclosed a hut about 5½ ft square with ridged
roof supported by two internal posts. Ordinary
dwellings may have been similar but larger

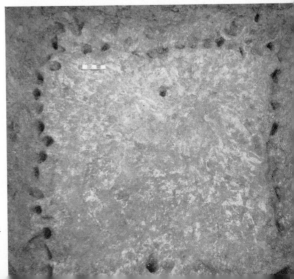

94

95 A Beaker cist burial from *Nether Criggie, Dunnottar, Kincardineshire*. This is unusual because it contains two individuals, a 20-year-old woman with two beakers and a new-born baby, presumably a childbirth death. The cist has lost its side slab; length about 3 ft; sunk 6 ft below ground

96 Burial of a Beaker leather-worker near *Amesbury, Wilts*, accompanied by a cup and his tools: copper awl, flint knife, antler implements, and with a wooden tool in his hand and a pointed wooden board over the body

97 A Beaker burial in wicker-lined pit at *Dorchester, Oxon*. Contracted bodies are characteristic, possibly bound with rope, and the position of grave goods often suggests that the dead were buried clothed

98

99

98 The bell-beaker and grave goods from *Dorchester,
Oxon.*: wristguard and two metal knives closely paralleled in south Germany. Bell-beakers are often thus
associated with archery equipment. Beaker $8\frac{1}{2}$ in. tall.
[AMO]

99 Grave goods associated with a bell-beaker at *Radley,
Berks.* The arrowheads are typical of the early second
millennium, and the gold ear-rings (nearly 2 in. long)
were in position as worn; the grave was that of a
young man. Possibly a late Beaker burial, *ca* seven-
teenth century BC. [AMO]

100 Gold ear-ring, one of a pair from *Orton, Morayshire,*
4 in. long. Others of this type, in gold or bronze,
occur in various parts of Britain; their ultimate origin
may lie in the east Mediterranean. Beaker culture.
[NMAS]

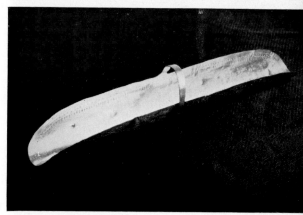

100

101

102

101 A battle-axe of Cornish tourmaline granite found with a necked beaker at *Woodhenge, Wilts.* Held in the hand of a male skeleton, it is nearly 6 in. long. Battle-axes and daggers are the normal armament associated with these beakers by contrast with the archery of the bell-beaker folk. [DM]

102 Grave goods from a necked beaker grave under a large 'bowl' barrow at *Amesbury, near Stonehenge, Wilts*: a whetstone and flint dagger (just over 7 in. long). The beaker is a fine, long-necked type with finger-nail ornament. [DM]

103 Knife-dagger (blade $3\frac{1}{2}$ in. long) with bone pommel from the grave of a 60-year-old man in a cemetery of pit burials at *Eynsham, Oxon.* The 'ghost' of the base of the wooden hilt can be seen on the dagger blade. The beaker is a degenerate necked type. [AMO]

103

104

104 The grave goods associated with two long-necked beakers from *Winterbourne Monkton, Wilts,* closely resemble those found with 'food vessels' in northern Britain and with some Wessex Culture graves: a 'pulley-ring' and two conical buttons of shale, a flint knife and piece of polished greenstone. Larger button nearly 3 in. diameter. [DM]

105 Tanged copper dagger, one of a pair of gold discs (right) and bell-beaker from a grave on *Mere Down, Wilts,* with a copy of a similar gold disc from *Monkton Farleigh, Wilts.* The discs with cruciform ornament may be 'sun symbols'. Discs about 1⅛ in. diam. [DM]

105

106 Flint daggers (longest 6½ in.) and a bone copy from the *London area*. Such flint pieces would have a wooden handle and leather sheath with straps, but must have been mainly for non-functional purposes. Beaker culture. [LM]

107 Handled flat dagger from *Corston Beacon, Pembrokeshire*, found with a male inhumation in a long stone cist of almost megalithic proportions. The pommel is missing, the wooden hilt being attached to the blade by three rivets. Blade now just over 7 in. long. Earlier Bronze Age. [NMW]

108

108 A trepanned skull from a Beaker burial under a barrow
on *Crichel Down, Dorset*. The operation, one of the
earliest surgical treatments known, was often success-
ful, but here proved fatal; it may have been carried
out to ease headaches or for ritual reasons. The dead
man also suffered from a spinal deformity

109 A Rinyo-Clacton henge monument at *Dorchester, Oxon.* There was originally an outer bank; the inner area, about 7 yds across, and the ditch sides contained 21 pit cremations with no grave goods. The holes at the base of each ditch segment seem to have been ritual

110 Henge monument at *Woodhenge, Wilts*; six oval settings of timber posts now marked by concrete stumps; possibly a roofed structure. A ritual child-burial lay in the centre. Rinyo-Clacton culture; maximum diameter nearly 50 yards. The rings were enclosed by a ditch with outer bank

111

112

111 A Beaker henge, *Arbor Low, Derbys*, with double entrance and a circle of 42 stones (the largest 13 ft high), now lying on the surface. Diameter over 80 yds

112 Part of the great henge monument, the *Ring of Brodgar, Orkney Mainland*, with a circle of (originally) 60 stones up to 15 ft high inside the ditch, and two entrances. Contrast the sea-level siting with that of Arbor Low at 1200 ft above sea level

113

113 The great circle at *Avebury, Wilts*, one of the two largest Beaker henges, about a quarter of a mile across and covering over 28 acres. Three and perhaps four entrances are original. The central area contains two small stone circles about 100 yds in diameter and other structures

114 The bank, internal ditch and great stone circle at *Avebury*. The ditch, now greatly silted, was about 30 ft deep and the bank about equally high. The circle

originally contained 100 stones of up to 60 tons, of local sarsen rock

115 The *Avebury Avenue* of about 100 pairs of stones running from the great circle along a winding route to a smaller henge monument on Overton Hill, some $1\frac{1}{2}$ miles distant. It has been suggested that alternating and opposite stones were male (tall and thin) and female (broad, trapezoid)

116 Stone circle on *Cleator Moor, Cumberland*. Such circles are widespread in highland Britain and may be isolated or associated with a variety of other ritual and burial features; local folk legend often attaches to them but little is known of their date and functions

117 Stone alignment on *Down Tor, Dartmoor*. Its length is about 380 yds, and the stones increase in height as it approaches the round barrow with stone kerb; tallest stone, adjoining the barrow, 9 ft 6 in. high (originally more). Probably early second millennium

118

119

Air photograph of barrow circles and a small cursus monument at *North Stoke, Oxon*, showing as colour markings in the growing crops. The cursus is about 12 yds wide and its parallel ditches run for about 250 yds, terminating by a long mortuary enclosure of Neolithic date

119 Air view of *Stonehenge, Wilts*, showing the Rinyo-Clacton henge monument surrounding the stone structures, the ditch-and-bank avenue running from it (about 25 yds across) and, in the distance, the great cursus disappearing into the plantation—the cursus is at over 100 yds wide, nearly 2 miles long and closed both ends

120

120 Aerial view of the central area of *Stonehenge*. Phase I (Rinyo-Clacton) comprised the outer ditch with its low inner bank and circle of 56 'Aubrey holes'—ritual pits. Phase II (Beaker) consisted of an uncompleted double circle of bluestones (pl. 121). Phase III, erected by the Wessex Culture in the seventeenth-fifteenth centuries BC, consisted of the present stone structures: an outer circle of 30 sarsen uprights carrying a continuous series of lintels, 100 ft in diameter and 16 ft high to the top of the lintels; a horseshoe-shaped setting of five trilithons graded in size up to the central trilithon standing 24 ft to the top of its now fallen lintel; and within each of these a circle and horseshoe-setting of bluestones respectively. The mortise-and-tenon and tongue-and-groove jointing of the lintels and their uprights can be seen in this plate and no. 122. The finesse of the whole masonry technique and precision of the layout are outstanding in this, the most spectacular prehistoric monument of Europe

121 The sockets and stumps of the unfinished and dismantled double bluestone circle at *Stonehenge* (Q and R holes) during excavation. Beaker culture

122 Part of the final stone structures at *Stonehenge*, of Wessex Culture date. Note the continuous curve of the lintels on the outer circle

121

122

123

124

23 *Carn Meini, Presely Mountains, Pembrokeshire,* the source of the 'bluestones' transported by the Beaker folk to Stonehenge, over 130 miles direct. The largest stone now weighs over 6 tons and the blocks must have been carried, probably by river and coastwise on rafts, and overland on rollers

24 Sarsen blocks lying on the ground on the *Marlborough Downs, N. Wiltshire,* whence the sarsen stones of Stonehenge would have been brought. The distance is only about 25 miles direct, but the stones weighed up to 50 tons or more, and transport of both these and the bluestones was an enormous undertaking in early second millennium times

25 Chalk axes from post sockets in the two outer circles of the henge at *Woodhenge, Wilts.* Deliberately buried and clearly unusable, they must be votive deposits of an axe cult. Larger nearly 4 in long. Rinyo-Clacton culture. [DM]

26 Jadeite axes from *Cambridgeshire.* These were possibly imported from Germany or Switzerland and are often obviously unused. Their importation may be linked with the beginning of metallurgy in the early second millennium BC. Longest 7 in. [CMAE]

27 A votive hoard of deliberately broken bronze axes from a barrow at *Jevington, Sussex;* of the same shape as the axe carvings at Stonehenge. Lengths from about 6 in. Earlier Bronze Age. [SML]

125

126

127

128

129

130

128 Carvings on one of the sarsen uprights in the outer circle of *Stonehenge*, representing a dagger, probably of E. Mediterranean (Mycenean) type, and numerous axes of British earlier Bronze Age form. Other enigmatical markings occur elsewhere at Stonehenge

129 Fragment of a stone block from the kerb of a cairn under a round barrow at *Badbury, Dorset*, bearing cup marks, two axe carvings of triangular shape and two dagger carvings (the longer about 1 ft) reminiscent of the Stonehenge dagger carving. Earlier Bronze Age

130 Carved stone from the end of a tongue-and-groove jointed cist at *Ri Cruin, Crinan, Argyll*, bearing carvings of many axes, some like those at Badbury, others closer to the Stonehenge ones. Slab about 18 in. square. [NMAS]

131 Rebated side-slab from a stone cist at *Badden, Lochgilphead, Argyll*, 5 ft long. The multiple lozenges recall passage grave art, but the tomb type here and at Ri Cruin (above) may derive from northern Europe along the metalworkers' trade routes. Earlier Bronze Age. [GLM]

132 Side slab from a megalithic cist with a cremation below a round barrow at *Pool Farm, Somerset*, bearing cup marks and foot carvings somewhat like those at the Calderstones (pl. 77). Earlier Bronze Age. [BCM]

133 Stone outcrop with cup-and-ring markings at *Drumtroddan, Wigtownshire*. Such symbols are not part of the passage grave repertoire but are found widely throughout Europe and the British Isles in connection with the early metal-workers and especially in Galicia

131

132

133

134 Part of a barrow cemetery on *Normanton Down, near Stonehenge, Wilts*. From the bottom there are: a bell barrow, a double bell (63 yds long), a disc (73 yds across), a bowl and a 'small long' barrow. Bell barrows often cover male graves of the Wessex Culture, disc ones female graves, while bowl barrows were used over a much longer period for graves of either sex

135 *Silbury Hill, near Avebury, Wilts*, the largest barrow in Europe, covering over 5 acres, 125 ft high and containing some half million cubic yards of earth derived from the broad quarry ditch here seen flooded. No burial or other structure has been discovered within it

36

37

138

36 Cemetery of Bronze Age barrows on *Snail Down*, *Wilts*, including bell, bowl and disc types and one 'pond' barrow. Beyond the barrows is a later Bronze Age ranch boundary ditch

37 Detail of the central area of the barrow in pl. 138, showing the debris from a pyre (foreground), the central pit which originally contained a cremation urn, and charred timbers

38 Bell barrow on *Snail Down* (arrowed on pl. 136), during excavation. Diameter of the ditch about 40 yds; barrow originally about 8 ft high. Earlier Bronze Age

39 Section of a barrow at *Wotton, Surrey*, with a mound of turves capped with stones. Barrows of all kinds are much more complicated structures than is apparent on the surface

139

14

14

14

143

144

140 Grave goods from *Bush Barrow, Normanton, Wilts*, found under a large bowl barrow with the extended inhumation of a Wessex Culture chief. The axe lay by the head, the daggers and scabbard hook by the right arm, a small dagger in the left hand, the mace with bone-inlaid wooden handle and the small gold lozenge by the legs and the large gold lozenge on the chest (*cf* the Barclodiad carving, pl. 73). Length of large lozenge 7 in. [DM (*electrotypes of the gold objects*)]

141 Wessex Culture grave goods from a tree-trunk coffin at *Hove, Sussex*. The cup, of amber probably from Jutland, is nearly 4 in. across; note the double-edged form of axe, possibly also with Scandinavian affinities. [BRM]

142 Grave group from the cist burial of a Wessex warrior under a bowl barrow at *Snowshill, Glos*. The pin is a central European type and the collared spearhead shows how this weapon developed from the dagger. Dagger 8½ in. long. [BM]

143-4 Greatly enlarged details of the gold-pin decoration of the hilt of one of the *Bush Barrow* daggers; the pins are 1/100 in. thick. Seen from above (143) and in section (144)

145 Mace-head of jet or shale studded with gold, found with an amber cup, gold plaque, dagger, 'incense cup' and urn in the grave of a Wessex chief at *Clandon, Dorset*. 3 in. across. [DCM]

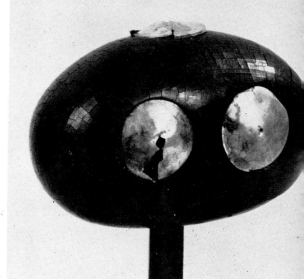

145

146 Grave goods from the cremated burial of a rich Wessex lady in the *Upton Lovell Golden Barrow, Wilts*. The multiple-strand necklace is of amber, the button of shale with a gold cover bearing a cruciform design on the round base; a knife, bodkin, hollow gold beads, two gold 'cones' and a finely incised gold plate accompanied the collared urn and 'grape cup'. Gold plate just over 6 in. long. [DM]

147 The crouched inhumation of an old lady in a bowl barrow on *Manton Down, Wilts*, was accompanied by this rich collection of grave goods; the 150 beads are of shale, and the gold ornaments comprise a gold-bound amber disc (perhaps a sun amulet), a miniature halberd pendant and a bead of shale bound with gold. Knife blade nearly 2 in. long. Wessex Culture. [DM]

148 Cup from a barrow at *Winterbourne Stoke, Wilts* (rim diameter just over 4 in.), and necklace from a bell barrow at *Upton Lovell, Wilts*. The beads include 10 segmented faience ones of east Mediterranean origin, eleven of Scandinavian amber and eleven of Dorset shale. Wessex Culture. [DM]

149 Gold cup from a cist inhumation under a barrow at *Rillaton, Cornwall*, accompanied by a dagger, beads and a pot. The form and corrugated ornament suggest that this was an actual import from Mycenean Greece, perhaps a gift to a Cornish chieftain. Height just over 3 in. Earlier Bronze Age. [BM]

150 Gold-ornamented pendants from Wessex Culture graves; the three bound amber discs may be sun symbols and have parallels in Mycenean Greece, the halberds suggest contacts with central Europe, and the 'horned' pendant may be related to bull-cults of the east Mediterranean. Discs about 1¾ in. diameter. [DM]

147

148

151 Earlier Bronze Age metalwork from sites in *Cambridgeshire*. It includes the earliest types of axe and spearhead, and (top left) a halberd blade for mounting at right-angles to a wooden shaft—either a weapon or a ritual object. The halberd is nearly 1 ft long. [CMAE]

152 Part of a hoard from *Arreton Down, Isle of Wight*, comprising axes, a dagger and two types of spearhead (one in cut-away modern shaft to show method of hafting). Larger axe 8 in. long. Fifteenth century BC. [BM]

153 Gold collar (lunula) from *Auchentaggart, Sanquhar, Dumfriesshire*. Such ornaments, in sheet gold, are common in Ireland and some imitate multi-strand bead necklaces and their spacers in their decoration. This specimen may have been made from the local gold ores from Leadhills. Nearly 9 in. diameter. Earlier Bronze Age. [NMAS]

154 Multi-strand crescentic necklace of jet, with spacer beads, from *Aberlemno, Angus*; these are the normal North British equivalents of Irish lunulae and Wessex amber necklaces. Mid-second millennium. [NMAS]

153

154

155

155 Chalk cylinders found by a child's grave under a round barrow at *Folkton, Yorks* (E.R.). Their decoration recalls passage grave art motifs and the Iberian 'eye' symbol occurs on each. Diameter of the largest $5\frac{1}{2}$ in., of the smallest 4 in. Earlier Bronze Age. [BM]

156 Bowl with gold ornament from a former lake at *Caergwrle, Flint*, presumably a votive deposit and perhaps representing a 'ship of the dead'. The finely incised concentric circles may imitate rows of shields (cf pl. 319), the pendant triangles oars, and the zigzags waves. A pair of 'eyes' occurs at each end. The bowl is oval, of wood or shale; length about 7 in. Possibly earlier Bronze Age. [NMW]

157 Grave goods from a cist burial in the *Knowes of Trotty, Orkney Mainland*, comprising parts of a multi-strand amber necklace (cf pl. 146) and fragments of two (originally four) gold discs of Irish type, 3 in. diameter, possibly the bases of button covers. Mid-second millennium. [NMAS]

56

57

158 Three variant forms of 'food vessel' vases from *Wales*. These derive their form and ornament from a mixture of later Neolithic styles, mainly Insular and Beaker. Centre vessel (a cast) is $7\frac{1}{2}$ in. tall. Earlier Bronze Age. [NMW]

159 Food vessels of Irish Bowl type from *Scotland*, deriving their shape and ornament mainly from Beaker originals. They accompany inhumations or cremations. Widths about $4\frac{1}{2}$–5 in. Earlier Bronze Age. [NMAS]

160 Collared urn and 'grape cup' accompanying an inhumation burial under a bowl barrow at *Normanton*, *Wilts*, together with beads and pendants. Such vessels also accompany cremations, and they develop into various types of cinerary urn. Urn 8 in. high. Wessex Culture. [DM]

161 Jar in the latest Insular Neolithic style from *West Kennet* long barrow, *Wilts*, with an overhanging 'collar' leading to the insular cinerary urn forms and with decoration combining Beaker and Rinyo-Clacton elements. Height about 8 in. Early second millennium. [DM]

160

161

162 A composite round barrow at *Tregulland, Cornwall*, during excavation. A central cist was surrounded, first by a double circle of stakes, then by a 'ring cairn' of stones, 3 ft high, buttressed with clay and capped with turves, and the whole encased in a stone cairn. Earlier Bronze Age

163 One of the stones from the *Tregulland* ring-cairn, bearing 'cup marks', ritual symbols known from graves and ritual sites of the earlier Bronze Age

164 A composite barrow at *Breach Farm, Llanbleddian, Glamorgan*. A pit cremation with bones of three individuals was covered by a mound of clay, turf and two cappings of clay, with a surrounding kerb of stones, 27 yds in diameter. Earlier Bronze Age

163

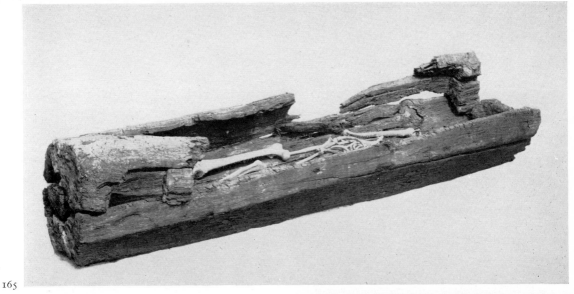

165

165 A finely-shaped tree-trunk coffin of oak containing an inhumation from *Chingford Reservoir, Essex*. Such coffins enclosed both inhumations and cremations in the earlier Bronze Age and are sometimes boat-like in shape. [LM]

166 The decayed remains of a timber coffin at *Milton Lilbourne, Wilts*, with a cremation accompanied by an 'incense cup' under a bell barrow. Earlier Bronze Age

167 Two cremations in enlarged food vessels at *Simondston, Bridgend, Glamorgan*. One of the cist slabs bore cup marks. Mid-second millennium

166

167

168

168 Cremation at *Liskey, Cornwall*, in a fine, large, 'Cornish' handled urn 16½ in. tall. Only token fragments of the burnt bones were enclosed. One of several graves in a composite bell barrow of turves, earth and stones. Earlier Bronze Age

169 Collared and biconical urns of the earlier Bronze Age from *Sussex* with a pigmy cup of collared form. These and many other types of cremation urn were used in the earlier and later Bronze Age. Urn at the back just over 1 ft high. [WM]

170 A selection of Welsh pigmy cups, diameters ranging from 2½ to 3 in. Some have perforated sides, others often two small holes, perhaps a memory of the 'eye' motif. The cruciform ornament on the base of one recalls the 'sun' symbols in gold. Earlier Bronze Age. [NMW]

169

170

171 Palstaves, the characteristic axe form during the later second millennium, showing the great variety of detailed shapes. Average length about 6 in. [CMAE]

172 Weapons of the later second millennium. The dagger has been developed into a longer dirk or rapier; the spearheads are socketed and often looped on the socket. Note the different sizes of spearhead, for javelins and lances; they range from 4 to 15 in. [CMAE]

173 Hoard of personal ornaments and tools from *Edington Burtle, Somerset*, indicating new contacts with northern Europe at the end of the second millennium. The objects include palstaves, sickles, bracelets, rings and collars. Axes about 6 in. long. [TM]

174 Another personal hoard of about 1200 BC, from *Barton Bendish, Norfolk*, including collars, bracelets, rings, palstaves and a great quoit-headed pin, 6 in. diam. [AMO]

175 Hoard of personal objects from *Blackrock, Brighton, Sussex*. The dirk hilt and ring bracelets are north German forms; the 'Sussex loop' armlets are a locally evolved type, continuing into the later Bronze Age. Dirk blade nearly 10 in. long. Late second millennium. [BRM]

171

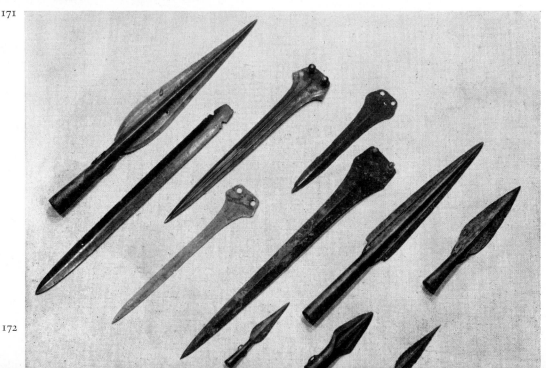

172

173

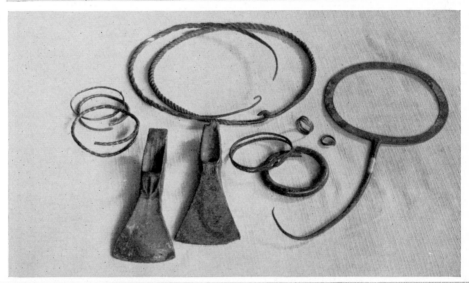

174

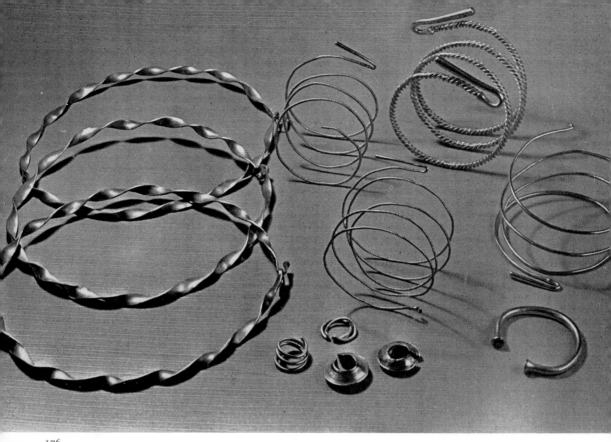

176

177

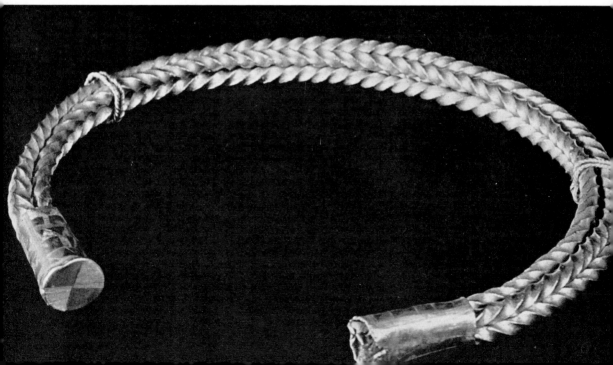

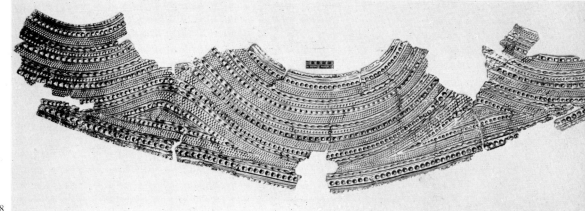

178

179

176 Gold ornaments from *Llanwrthwl, Brecknock; Great Orme, Caernarvon* and *Knighton, Radnorshire.* The ribbon torcs would be necklets, the spiral-coiled ones bracelets. The solid bracelet and penannular 'lock rings' (*cf* pl. 205) are later Bronze Age, the others dating from the later second millennium. Diam. of the ribbon torcs about 8 in. [NMW]

177 Massive gold collar from *Moulsford, Berks*, weight about 1 lb. Made of four twisted rods with terminals of incised sheet gold bearing a cruciform design at their ends in the earlier Bronze Age tradition. Diam. about 7 in. About 1400 BC. [RM]

178 A highly decorated gold cape from a male inhumation cist under a cairn at *Mold, Flint*, found with about 300 amber beads and cloth. The sheet, extended, measures about 3 ft 6 in. and weighs over 1 lb. Late second millenium BC. [BM]

179 Detail of the repoussé ornament on the *Mold* cape, in imitation of rows of beads of various forms. [BM]

180 Reconstruction of the *Mold* cape as worn, attached to backing of cloth or leather; chest ornaments in beadwork of comparable form are known from Egypt. *Drawing by B. Hope-Taylor*

180

181 Scottish 'encrusted urns', a type evolved from food vessels especially in northern and western Britain in the late second and early first millennium. About 15 in. tall. [NMAS]

182 A selection of later Bronze Age 'bucket urns' from a cemetery at *Ardleigh*, *Essex*, with over 100 burials in groups. Such vessels were used for domestic as well as burial purposes. Heights from 10 to 20 in. [CEM]

183 Globular cremation urns from a cemetery in the *Deverel Barrow*, *Dorset*, with over 20 burials, mostly in pits with stone covers. Later Bronze Age. Tallest urn 10 in. [BCM]

184 Pottery from a later Bronze Age farmstead on *Thorny Down*, *Wilts*, showing close similarity to the burial urns in the previous plate. Larger 9½ in. tall. [SM]

181

182

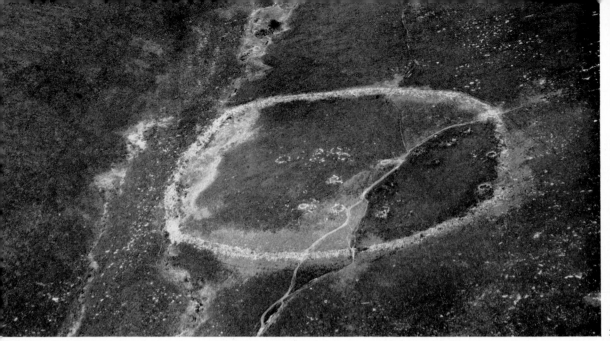

185 *Grimspound, Dartmoor, Devon*, a cattle enclosure and settlement of nearly 4 acres; the perimeter wall, 9–10 ft thick, enclosed 16 huts, 7 other buildings and 5 cattle pens, the latter built up against its inner face. Later Bronze Age

186 Celtic field system on *Preshute Down, Wilts*, partly of later Bronze Age date. The small cattle enclosure (arrowed) is about 45 by 50 yds across and is earlier than the adjoining fields, though still later Bronze Age

187 Hut circle at *Merrivale, Dartmoor, Devon*. The stone walls would originally have stood about 4½ ft high,

enclosing an area up to about 20 ft across and supporting a conical roof of thatch or turf. Later Bronze Age

188 Post-sockets for a timber-framed, circular hut with a porched entrance on the far side, at *Itford Hill, Sussex*, typical of the lowland areas of southern Britain. The walls would be filled with clay-faced wattle panels. Later Bronze Age

189 Reconstructed drawing of the settlement on *Itford Hill*, the several groups of huts housing a single social unit. Note the unusual communal cooking place sited away from the huts. *Drawing by Patrick Burke*

190

191

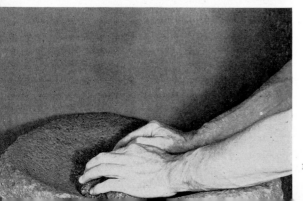

192

190 The head and stilt of an oak plough from *Milton Loch, Kirkcudbrightshire*, from above and side. An oak share would fit under the head and the top of the stilt would project through a mortise in the great beam to which the oxen were yoked. Ploughs of this type were probably used in the later Bronze Age and Iron Age; this is second century AD. Overall length about 4 ft

191 Scratch marks from the tip of a ploughshare at *Gwithian, Cornwall*, dating from the earlier Bronze Age; the oldest yet found in Britain. The ploughing in two directions, at right-angles, may be due to work in different years or to the breaking down of autumn furrows by cross-ploughing in spring

192 Quern of 'saddle' type from *Cock Hill, Worthing, Sussex*. Corn-grinding mills of this kind were used during the Bronze and earlier Iron Ages by rubbing the upper stone backwards and forwards. Length 20 in. [SML]

193 Textile fragments found with a cremated burial at *Amesbury, near Stonehenge, Wilts*. Linen or other vegetable fibres may have been woven in Neolithic times; wool was in use throughout the second millennium and later. [SM]

194 A large storage jar, small cup (a copy) and cylindrical loom-weights of Later Bronze Age date from *Sussex*. The weights, weighing up to 3 or 4 lbs, were used to keep the vertical threads hanging taut on an upright loom; they are of fired clay. Height of jar 14 in., cup 2½ in. [BRM]

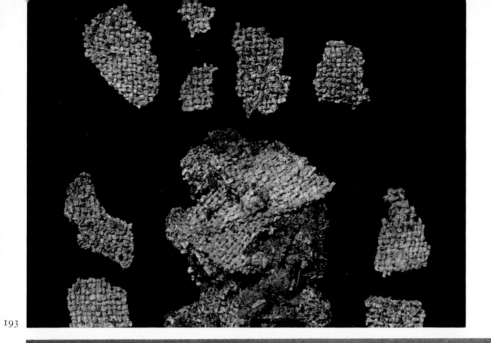

193

194

195 Dug-out canoe of oak from *Llangorse, Brecknock*, with a beaked prow and cut-away seat in the stern. Such canoes were used throughout prehistoric times from the Mesolithic period onwards; some were hollowed by fire, others carved with adzes. Length over 15 ft. Probably later Bronze Age. [NMW]

196 Prow of a dug-out canoe from *Scotland*, strongly carved into the form of an animal head, perhaps a bovid. Compare the shape of the prow of the miniature boat, pl. 319. Probably later Bronze Age. [NMAS]

197 The remains, as found, of an elaborately constructed, plank-built boat from *N. Ferriby, Yorks* (E.R.), showing the keel, part of the lowest starboard side strake, and the cleats and bars holding the three keel planks. Later Bronze Age

198 Model of the *N. Ferriby* boat as found. There would have been three strakes on either side giving a total length of about 50 ft. and a maximum beam of about 8 ft, doubtless with cross-struts and seats for oarsmen. A superb example of early ship-building; the timbers were very carefully jointed, held together by sewing with yew withies and caulked. [NMM]

196

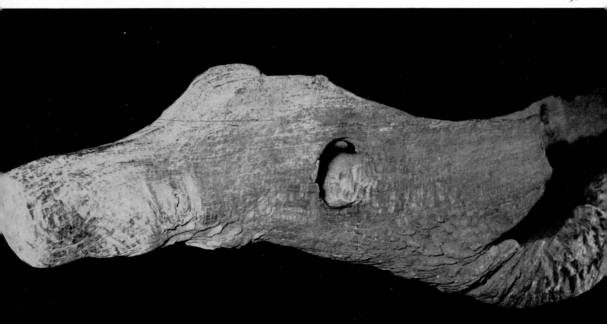

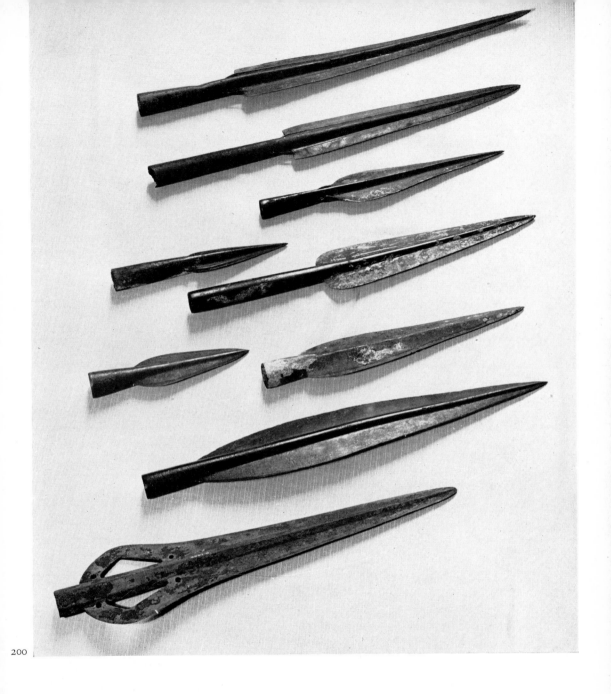

200

199 Swords of the later Bronze Age from the *Thames*.
The bottom (28 in. long) is an imported prototype
from which native forms developed (centre); the top
sword is a later, intrusive ('carp's tongue') type of
the eighth and seventh centuries. [LM]

200 Later Bronze Age spearheads from the *Thames*, showing again the wide range of different kinds of such
weapons: lances, javelins and spears. Lengths from 7
to 20 in. [LM]

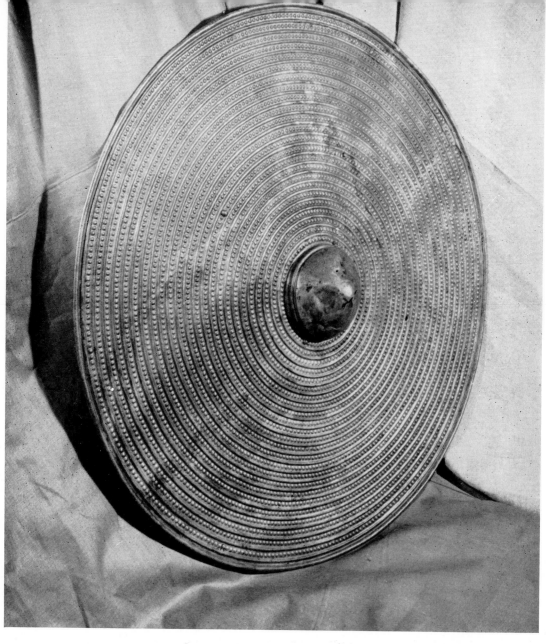

201 Sheet-bronze shield from *Yetholm, Roxburghshire.*
Thin metal shields such as this, sometimes found as
votive offerings in former lakes and rivers, could only
have been for ceremonial uses; functional ones would
be made of leather shaped on wooden moulds. Diam.
2 ft. Eighth century BC. [NMAS]

202 Bucket of sheet bronze from *Cardross, Dunbartonshire.*
It stands over 18 in. high and represents the introduc-
tion of sheet metal containers into Britain from W.
Europe in the eighth and seventh centuries BC. [NMAS]

203 Cauldron of sheet bronze with the rivets performing
an ornamental as well as a structural function; such
cauldrons might hold 10 or more gallons and when
full could hardly have been carried by the ring
handles; they may have been ceremonial no less than
functional. Maximum diam. 2 ft. From the *West of
Scotland.* Seventh century BC. [NMAS]

202

203

204

204 Gold bracelets of later Bronze Age type from *Patcham, Sussex*. One is a cheap imitation, perhaps passed off as solid, with a bronze core plated with gold. Nearly 3 in. diam. [BRM]

205 Later Bronze Age ornaments of gold and bronze from *Scotland*. The open, solid rings may have been a form of currency, the wide-ended ones dress fasteners and the open ones of triangular section ('lock rings') were possibly worn in the hair. The pin is over 7 in. long. [NMAS]

206 Socketed axes of various regional types; the hafted specimen is from *Co. Westmeath, Ireland*. Some of the axes are too thin or too small to have been functional and may have been another form of currency. Length of the Irish handle 14 in. Later Bronze Age. [CMAE]

207 Part of a hoard of scrap metal and miscellaneous objects from *Fen Reach, Cambs*, including both objects of native type and elements of the 'carp's tongue' complex. Seventh century BC. [AMO]

205

206

207

208 Axe moulds of various types from *Scotland*. The open mould (top) (length nearly 6 in.) is the earliest and would be suitable for casting copper; the two-piece stone mould was used for bronze—the pair for socketed axes and the half (lower) for palstaves. The model of an axe as cast shows the casting 'jet' still attached to the axe mouth. [NMAS]

209 A bronze founder's stock-in-trade from *Minster, Kent*, with scrap objects, metal cakes and the by-products of casting. Such founders would be itinerant, making goods as required from obsolete objects. [BM]

210 Two-piece stone mould for a spearhead (length about 7 in.) and fragments of clay moulds used for swords; note the wood graining on the right-hand fragment from the wooden model round which the clay mould was formed. Later Bronze Age. Various sites in *Scotland*. [NMAS]

211 Later Bronze Age casting equipment. The bronze moulds were used for making wax or lead models; these would be encased in clay and fired, the wax melting and leaving a matrix for the bronze for the final object. This 'lost wax' method permitted much more rapid mass-production. Length of 'tongs' about 15 in. [BM]

210

211

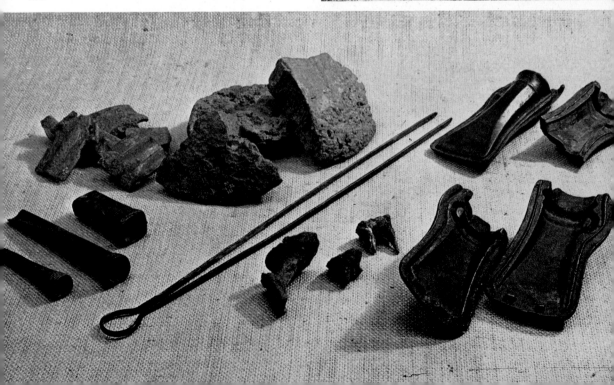

212

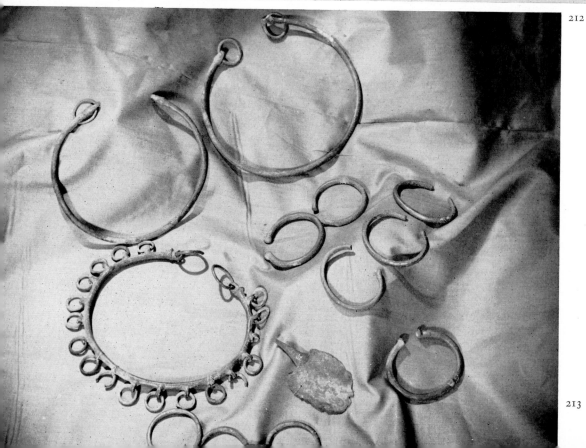

213

212 Hoard from *Welby, Leics*, containing horse-harness fittings (strap discs), handle attachments for a bowl and a small bronze cup, all of central European types, besides native objects. Early seventh century. Spearhead 8 in. long. [LEM]

213 Hoard of bronze personal ornaments from the *Braes of Gight, Aberdeens*, comprising a razor, bracelets and elaborate necklets, nearly 7 in. in diameter, one with hanging ringlets. Possibly imported by immigrants from N.W. Europe early in the seventh century BC. [NMAS]

214 Part of a hoard from a possible lake-side settlement at *Llyn Fawr, Glamorgan*, including one of two sheet bronze cauldrons, horse harness ornaments and other fittings, various tools and weapons together with three items of iron: spearhead and sickle imitating native types and imported sword (all bottom right). Early sixth century BC. Harness discs 6-7 in. diam. [NMW]

215 Fragment of the iron sword and hilt from the *Llyn Fawr* hoard—the earliest yet found in Britain. Overall length 10½ in. Sixth century BC. [NMW]

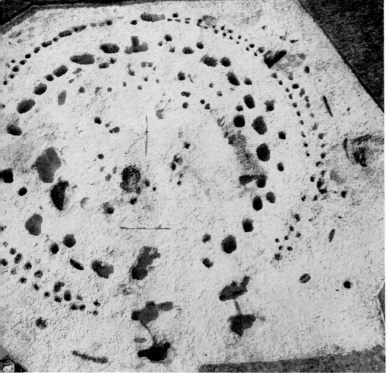

216

217

218

219

216 Post sockets of two superimposed houses (hence the double rows) inside an 11-acre enclosure at *Pimperne, Dorset*. The outer wall, 14 yds in diameter, was of slender timbers, the roof being supported by an inner ring of massive posts; in the foreground the sockets for a porched entrance. Iron Age A

220

217 The site of a lakeside dwelling (crannog) at *Milton Loch, Kirkcudbrightshire*; the house and its small harbour were joined to the shore by a 30-yd causeway. Second century AD

218 Reconstruction of the *Milton Loch* house, similar in size and form to the Pimperne and other large houses of the Iron Age 'Little Woodbury' economy. Diameter about 13 yds, with internal partitions. *Model by M. E. and J. G. Scott*

219 Rock-cut bedding trench for the outer, solid timber, wall of a large round house at *W. Brandon, Co. Durham*; about 17 yds across, with external eaves supports. The house stood in a 1 acre protected enclosure. Third–second centuries BC

220 View of a 'wheelhouse' at *Sollas, N. Uist*, during excavation. This type of building, the stone equivalent of the large circular timber house further south, occurs mainly in N. Scotland and the Northern and Western Isles. The radial piers and walls supported a roof covering the whole inner space; there is a central hearth. Early centuries AD

221 Interior of a 'wheelhouse' at *Jarlshof, Shetland*, about 24 ft diam., showing the original lintelled entrance (extreme left) and later entrance cut through the wall. The piers project about 6 ft into the interior forming alcoves about 10 ft high, and begin to oversail inwards at the base of the partly corbelled roof. Early centuries AD

221

222

222 The stone-built village at *Chysauster, Cornwall*, with four pairs of houses astride a central road. Each house had an unroofed courtyard with side rooms built into the thickness of the wall and, beyond, a roofed dwelling area with a hearth. Latest Iron Age

223 An underground storage chamber (fogou) at *Carn Euny, Cornwall*, leading from a settlement. It is 22 yds long (the far roof has collapsed) and opens in the middle on to a round, buried chamber. Height of fogou about 6 ft. Latest Iron Age

224 Storage pits at *Maiden Castle, Dorset*, used for keeping food (grain or meat) and, when contaminated, filled with domestic refuse. Some were lined with basket-work or stone. Characteristic of the 'Little Woodbury' mixed-farming economy. Iron Age A

225 The post-holes and bedding trenches of an Iron Age A temple at *Heathrow, Middlesex* inside an enclosed area about 150 yards across, also containing dwelling houses. The central rectangular shrine measures 6 by 5 yds and the enclosing colonnade and porch about 10 by 12 yds

226 Reconstructed drawing of the *Heathrow* settlement and temple, the latter bearing a close resemblance to the form of a classical temple. *Drawing by Alan Sorrell*

223

22

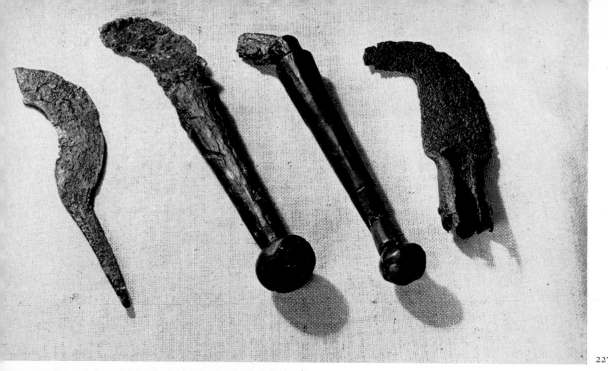

227

228

227 Farming equipment of iron from *Glastonbury, Somerset*, including a broken sickle, two handled leaf-knives and a billhook (length 10 in.) First century BC. [GM]

228 Ploughshare tip and billhook from the *Caburn, Sussex*; billhook 8½ in. long. The share tip would be suitable for light, stony soils; broader ones for medium, stone-free soils were introduced in Belgic areas at the end of the Iron Age. [SML]

229 Rotary quern from *Goodwood, Sussex*. These portable versions of the large powered mills of the classical world were introduced as a domestic labour-saving device into Britain in the first century BC. [SML]

230 Carpentry tools from *Glastonbury, Somerset*: gouge, files, awl and awl handles, small saw and large, wooden handled saw with an overall length of 16 in. Axes were not used, surprisingly, but instead adzes formed the standard tool of the carpenter. Iron Age B. [GM]

231 Three-footed wooden tub built up of staves bound with a metal band (the present hoop is modern), from *Glastonbury, Somerset*. Diam. 7 in. Iron Age B. [GM]

229

230

231

2

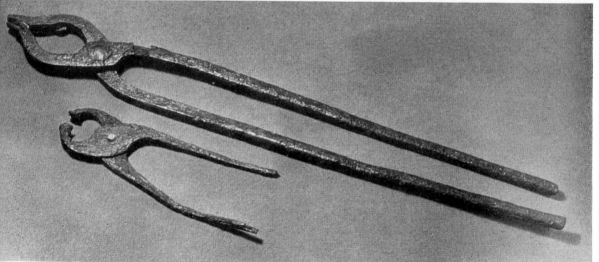

2

234

232 Blacksmith's bowl furnace from *W. Brandon, Co. Durham*. It is 1 ft diam. and 8 in. deep, with a groove for the nozzle of the bellows, and was originally covered with a clay dome. Used for reducing iron ore to produce a 'bloom' from which to forge wrought-iron equipment. Celtic Iron Age

233 Blacksmith's tongs from *Llyn Cerrig Bach, Anglesey*, identical in form to their modern equivalents. Longer tongs about 21 in. Celtic Iron Age. [NMW]

234 Socketed iron axe from the *Thames*. The smith has tried to imitate a cast, socketed bronze axe in wrought iron with a welded loop, perhaps to meet the conservative preference of a customer. Length 5 in. Earlier Iron Age [LM]

235

235 Iron Age weaving equipment from the *Somerset Lake Villages*. The clay loomweights weigh up to about 7 lbs; spindle whorls (one on a reconstructed spindle) are of clay, stone or bone; the perforated toe bones of sheep were probably bobbins for shuttles, and the combs were used to pack the woven cloth tightly on the loom. Largest comb 7½ in. long. [TM]

238

236 Coarse storage and cooking jars from *All Cannings Cross, Wilts*; note the close similarity to later Bronze Age urns of the two right-hand vessels. Tallest pot 18 in. high. Iron Age A. Fifth century BC. [DM]

237 Table ware from *All Cannings Cross*, including vessels with burnished red (haematite) or black surface, the small front vessel decorated with finely incised lines

after firing. Note the indentation in the base of the right-hand vessel. Front vessel nearly 4 in. diam. Iron Age A. Fifth century BC. [DM]

238 Fine decorated wares from the *Somerset Lake Villages*, still hand-made and ornamented in Celtic Art styles. Height of the tall storage jar 14 in. Iron Age B. Second–first centuries BC. [TM]

239

240

241

242

239 Bowls and 'saucepan' vessels from the *Somerset Lake Villages*, showing the incised decoration and fine, well-fired fabric. Bottom left: 6 in. diam. Iron Age B. Second–first centuries BC. [TM]

240 Copy of a bronze bowl from *Glastonbury, Somerset*; hammered from a sheet of bronze. Maximum diameter nearly 5 in., capacity about 1 pint. Iron Age B. [TM]

241 Cylindrical bone object, possibly a dice box, and dice from *Glastonbury, Somerset*. The dice have the 3, 4, 5 and 6 spots on their long sides. Box 3 in.; dice just under 1 in. long. Iron Age B. [GM]

242 Tankard from *Trawsfynnydd, Merioneth*. Built of 10 wooden staves with inset base, sheathed in sheet bronze running over the lip into the top of the interior, and with a fine handle in Celtic style. Height just over 5½ in., capacity about 3 pints. Iron Age B. First century AD. [CLM]

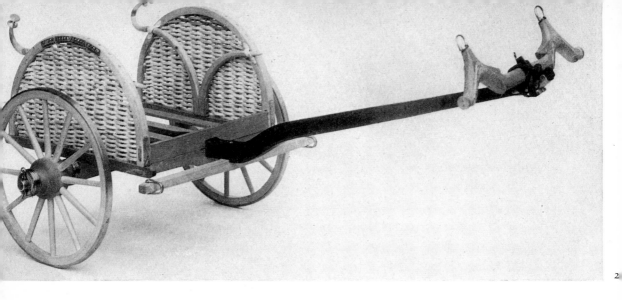

243 Model of an Iron Age chariot, lightly built with wicker sides and wheels 2 ft 6 in. to 3 ft diam., with shrunk-on iron tyres. The fittings include metal nave hoops, linch pins, pole sheath where the yoke joins, rein rings and decorative panels. Drawn by two ponies. Iron Age B. [NMW]

244 Unfinished oak wheel hub, turned on the lathe, and a number of spokes. Nave rim about 5-6 in. diam.; spokes $12\frac{1}{2}$-15 in. in overall length. *Glastonbury, Somerset.* Iron Age B. [GM]

45

45 Harness and chariot fittings from *Polden Hill, Somerset* and *Westhall, Suffolk*. They include rein rings (terrets), toggles or cheek pieces for bridle bits, linch pin caps, harness ornaments and a two-piece 'brooch' possibly for a horse-blanket. All were inlaid with enamel and glass. Brooch 6½ in. long overall. Iron age B. First century AD. [BM]

46 Cap for one of the two horns gripped while mounting a chariot, from the Thames at *Brentford, Middlesex*. The ornament is in the continental Celtic style from which British Celtic art developed. Perhaps an early third century import. Top diam. 3 in. [LM]

47 A pair of bridle-bits from *Ringstead, Norfolk*, of iron rings plated with sheet bronze and solid bronze links, decorated with plastic Celtic Art motifs. Overall lengths 10¼ in. First century BC. [NCM]

246

47

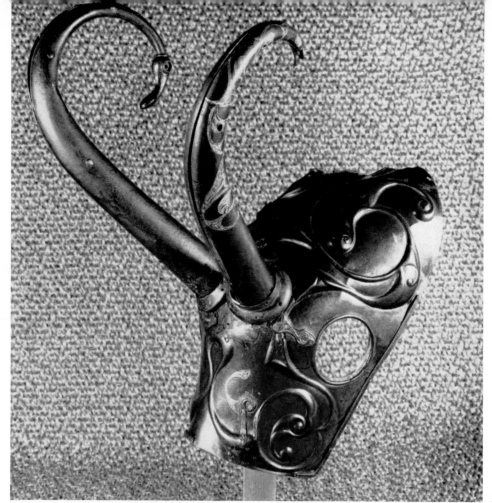

248

249

250

251

252

248 Composite object from *Torrs, Kirkcudbrightshire*. The horns were originally separate and formed the terminals of drinking horns. The remaining cap would fit over the ears on the head of a pony and probably had a plume on top. About 8 in. tall, the horns projecting about 7 in. Late third century BC. [NMAS]

249 Detail of the ornament on one of the *Torrs* horns, belonging to an early phase of Insular Celtic Art and paralleled by the Witham and Wandsworth shield parts (pl. 252-256). [NMAS]

250 Detail of the bird's head terminal of one of the *Torrs* horns (2 in. long); the eyes were originally filled with coral studs held with rivets. [NMAS]

251 Bronze shield-cover for parade use, from the Thames at *Battersea*, dating from about the Birth of Christ, when Roman provincial art was already beginning to influence native Celtic styles. The rigid, fold-over ornament contrasts sharply with the free-flowing lines of the earlier phases as in the following examples. Length just over 2 ft 6 in. [BM]

252 Bronze shield-cover from the *R. Witham, Lincs*, of early second century BC date. The faint outline can be traced of a now disappeared appliqué figure of a highly stylized boar. Length 3 ft 8 in. [BM]

253 Detail of the lower roundel of the *Witham* shield, with both plastic and linear decoration in the early Celtic style; note the conventionalized bird's head at the end of the central rib. [BM]

254 Shield boss from the Thames at *Wandsworth*, the central grip-cover bearing chased ornament and the outer rim a bold plastic pattern with superimposed linear designs. Overall diam. about 1 ft. [BM]

255

255 Central grip-cover of the *Wandsworth* shield boss, showing the chased designs including a bird's head like those in relief on the outer rim. Diam. of the cover nearly 4 in. [BM]

256 Detail of the chased ornament on the rim of the *Wandsworth* shield boss. Overall length of the linear design just under 3 in. [BM]

256

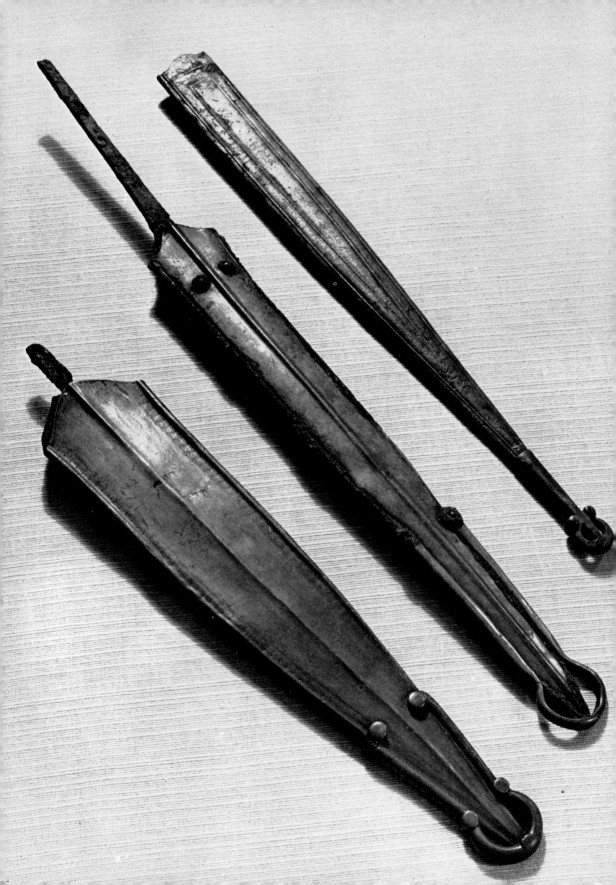

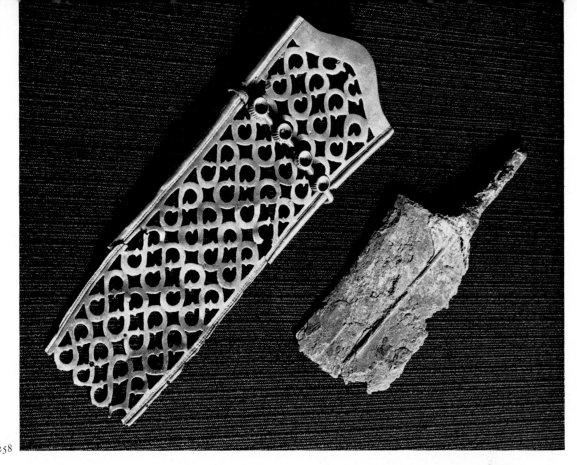

258

257 Daggers and bronze sheaths of the fourth century BC
from the Thames at *London*, possibly indicating a
local colony of immigrant warriors. Lengths of
sheaths and terminal chapes 10½–12½ in. [LM]

258 A magnificent openwork bronze covering for a
sheath and part of the iron dagger from *Hammersmith*.
The running S's are continental in style but the sheath
is probably of British manufacture. Surviving length
of the cover 6½ in. Perhaps fourth century BC. [LM]

259 Bronze hilt on an iron-bladed dagger from *Yorkshire*. The hilt, length about 4 in., is in the form of a
mannikin, his arms and legs forming the upper and
lower guards and his body the grip. First century BC.
[BM]

259

260 Views of front and back of the scabbard and of the iron-bladed sword with bronze hilt fittings from *Embleton, Cumberland*. This is a late, northern British type of the later first century AD. Original overall length about 2 ft. [BM]

261 Hilt of an iron-bladed sword from *Hod Hill, Dorset*, with bronze fittings to hold the grip-plates which would be of wood, bone or ivory. Hilt about 5 in. long. First century AD. [BM]

262 Openwork scabbard chape with chased ornament, the background filled in with a 'basketwork' design typical of the first century BC. The scabbard would be of wood, perhaps with iron or bronze covering plates. Length 6½ in. *Little Wittenham, Berks*. Iron Age B. [RM]

262

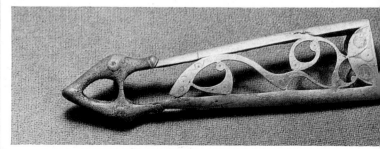

263

263 Miniature sword and shield from *Frilford, Oxon.*, found in a pit within a henge-like Iron Age ritual site underlying a Romano-British circular temple. The shield is of normal continental La Tène type; the sword suggests acquaintance with Roman weapons. Present length of sword 3 in. Celtic Iron Age. [AMO]

264 Bronze helmet cover from the *Thames*, of an unique horned type. The studs would have held bosses of red enamel and the whole, perhaps gilded, would have formed a parade head-dress. Nearly 17 in. from tip to tip of the horns. Probably first century BC. [BM]

264

265

266

265 Bronze brooches from various sites in *Wiltshire*, representing different fashions throughout the Iron Age; used to fasten clothing, especially the cloak at the neck. All about 2 in. long. [DM]

266 Personal and costume jewellery from *Meare, Somerset*, including brooches, pins, finger rings and bangles of shale and bronze. Bangle on extreme right 2 in. diam. Iron Age B. [TM]

267 Massive armlets and three snake bracelets from *Scotland*, where these represent a local development continuing into the Roman period. Snake bracelets about 3 in. diam. Northern Iron Age. [NMAS]

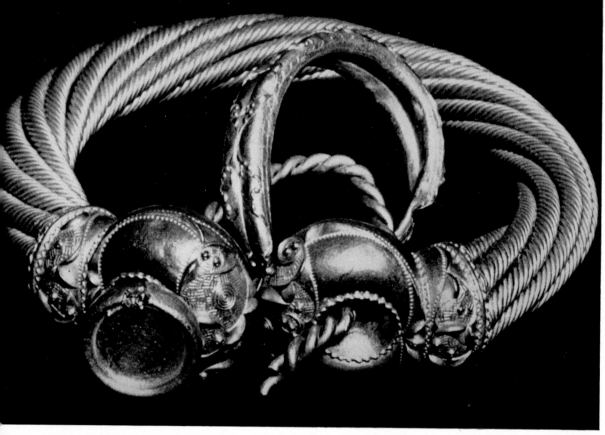

268 Part of a hoard of gold-alloy ornaments and other items from *Snettisham, Norfolk*. The great multi-strand electrum collar with elaborately decorated ring terminals is about 8 in. in diameter. Buried during the troubled times of the first century BC. Iron Age B. [NCM]

269 Two gold-alloy collars from *Ulceby, Lincs*, part of a hoard. Collars such as these and the Snettisham examples would be for ceremonial and probably religious wear. First century BC. Diameter of the larger 6 in. internally. Iron Age B. [AMO]

270

270 A poor man's iron collar and parts of necklaces of tusks, teeth and beads from *Meare* and *Ham Hill*, *Somerset*. The tusks, about 5 in. long, may reflect the ritual importance of the boar in Iron Age times. Iron Age B. [TM]

271 Bronze collar from *Wraxall, Somerset*, with cast relief ornament; the holes would have contained glass or enamel studs. Overall diam. nearly 7 in. First century A.D. [BCM]

272 Hinged bronze collar, secured by a pin at the front, from *Stichill, Roxburghshire*. Probably of Roman date. Internal diam. about 4 in. [NMAS]

273 Sheet bronze ceremonial collar for mounting on leather or cloth from the votive deposit in the lake of *Llyn Cerrig Bach, Anglesey*, perhaps a Druidic sacred site. Internal diam. nearly 4 in. Iron Age B. Perhaps first century BC. [NMW]

274 Bronze mirror, possibly from *S.E. England*, in the Mayer Collection. The design is worked on the back of the mirror; the front was highly polished. A fine example of the early mirror style with basketwork hatching. Iron Age B. First century BC. [CLM]

275 Part of a shield boss from *Tal-y-llyn, Merioneth*, with a triskele design executed in relief. Roundel nearly 3 in. diam. Second century BC. [NMW]

276 Part of a panel from the same shield showing how the Celtic artist tried to produce a plastic effect in a two-dimensional, chased technique. Roundel just over 3 in. diam. [NMW]

274

275

276

277

278

279

280

281

277 Hill-fort on *Ladle Hill, Hants*, uncompleted, showing how the upper levels from the ditches were heaped behind the line of the ramparts; these were to have a core of deep-quarried chalk and the top soil would be kept for use later as a capping

278 Single-rampart hill-fort on *Burrough Hill, Leics*, enclosing over 10 acres. There was a guard house on one side of the deep inturned entrance; a track from the far corner leads to a spring on the hillside

279 A great multiple-ramparted hill-fort on *Hambledon Hill. Dorset*, with a complicated history of enlargement and strengthening of the defences. Hut plat-

forms can be seen in the interior and a Neolithic bank barrow crowns the centre of the hill. Total area enclosed, about 25 acres

280 A fine Wessex hill-fort covering nearly 30 acres— *Yarnbury, Wilts*. The entrance is protected by complex outworks, and is itself inturned. The slight marks of an earlier stock-enclosure can be seen in the interior

281 A hill-slope fort at *Clovelly Dykes, Devon*; one of the great stock enclosures of the West Country and S. Wales. It covers 23 acres and has easy access to water and grazing lands; the settlement would be in the innermost enclosure

282

283

282 View showing the massive scale of the defences of *Maiden Castle, Dorset*, enclosing altogether 45 acres and dwarfing the huts and human and animal figures. This was probably a local tribal capital, and was stormed and sacked by Vespasian in about 47 AD

283 Part of the defences of the east entrance to *Maiden Castle*, showing the face of the rampart partly cleared, with sockets for upright timbers. The figures give the scale; in one phase there was a smooth 40° slope of no less than 80 ft from the bottom of the ditch to the top of the rampart

284 Part of a hoard of over 20,000 slingstones, one of several such ammunition stores at *Maiden Castle*. The introduction of sling warfare may be one of the reasons for the multiplication of rampart and ditch systems of hill-fort defence

284

285 Reconstruction of part of the defences of the fort at *Bindon, Dorset,* where the ramparts would be faced with vertical timber revetments and tied with timber struts. Enormous quantities of timber would be required for this purpose and for the dwellings inside the fort

286 Reconstruction drawing of the entrance and interior of a stone-ramparted hill-fort, *Llanmelin, Monmouth.* Note the gateway with sentry walk above and the vulnerability of attackers moving up the inturned entrance. *Drawing by Alan Sorrell*

285

286

287

288

289

287 The broch of *Mousa, Shetland*; a heavily defended farmstead dominating its coastal strip of land. In its restored condition it stands over 40 ft high, with walls 15 ft thick at the base enclosing a central area about 20 ft across. Early centuries AD

288 *Dun Telve* broch, *Glenelg, Inverness-shire*, standing to over 30 ft and showing the double-skin construction of the walls with tie-slabs at intervals. Some kind of roofed structure, perhaps of more than one storey, would occupy the central area. Early centuries AD

289 The stairs within the thickness of the wall of the *Mousa* broch; they would climb spirally from the ground floor to the top of the tower

290 War cemetery at *Sutton Walls, Hereford*. The victims of an assault on the hill-fort, possibly by a Belgic army, were thrown into the ditch; they are all young men and youths and many had been beheaded (bottom left) or otherwise mutilated, while others carried both fresh and ancient, healed wound marks

291 Part of a gang-chain from *Lord's Bridge, Barton, Cambs*. Altogether it is 12 ft long with six collars at 2 ft intervals. Used for transporting prisoners for sale as slaves, one of Britain's main pre-Roman exports. Each collar is about 5 in. across and can be opened only by releasing all the collars in front and passing them and the chain through a wide link. Belgic Iron Age. [CMAE]

290

291

292

293

294

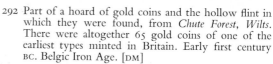

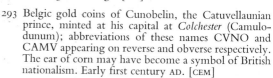

292 Part of a hoard of gold coins and the hollow flint in which they were found, from *Chute Forest, Wilts.* There were altogether 65 gold coins of one of the earliest types minted in Britain. Early first century BC. Belgic Iron Age. [DM]

293 Belgic gold coins of Cunobelin, the Catuvellaunian prince, minted at his capital at *Colchester* (Camulodunum); abbreviations of these names CVNO and CAMV appearing on reverse and obverse respectively. The ear of corn may have become a symbol of British nationalism. Early first century AD. [CEM]

294 Silver coins of Tasciovanus (lower) and his son Cunobelin (upper) from the end of the first century BC and the beginning of the first AD, from *Colchester.* The boar was a Celtic ritual animal (*cf* pls. 252, 313-315), and the obverse of the Cunobelin coin shows direct imitation of a Roman 'type'. [CEM]

295 Part of a hoard of 360 coins and the pot in which they lay, from *Sunbury-on-Thames, Middlesex.* These coins would be small change, made of a tin-bronze alloy by casting instead of striking. Current from the mid-

296

296 Belgic pottery from *Colchester* and *Lexden, Essex*. These wheel-thrown, mass-produced vessels include a great variety of kitchen and table wares; those shown here are a large, lidded storage jar (1 ft max. diam), a pedestal cup with lid, a platter and a pedestal urn. [CEM]

297 Lathe-turned vessels of shale from *Bedfordshire, Essex* and *Cambridgeshire*: a pedestal urn (15 in. tall), bowl and footed bowl (tazza). Belgic Iron Age. First century AD. [CMAE]

297

301

298 A rich burial from the Belgic cemetery at *Aylesford, Kent*. The stave-built bucket contained the cremated bones and was accompanied by pottery vessels, three brooches and a wine jug and ladle of bronze, the last two being imports. Height of bucket 10 in. [BM]

299 The *Aylesford* bucket showing the handle attachments and the decorated upperband with two opposed horses similar in style and detail to the chalk-cut figure at Uffington (pl. 307). [BM]

300 Detail of a handle mount on the *Aylesford* bucket in the form of a typical Celtic face with horned or plumed head-dress (*cf* pls. 310, 312)

301 A rich Belgic grave group from a woman's burial at *Colchester, Essex*, containing the traditional pedestal urn, other pottery vessels including two imported handled jugs, a bronze pin, a spun-bronze cup with enamel-studded handle and a mirror with engraved ornament. Jugs about 13 in. tall. [CEM]

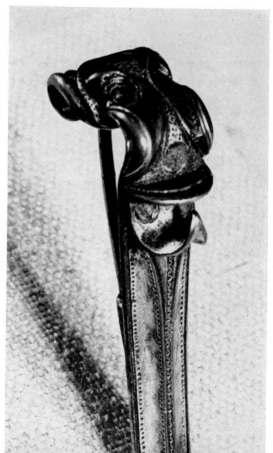

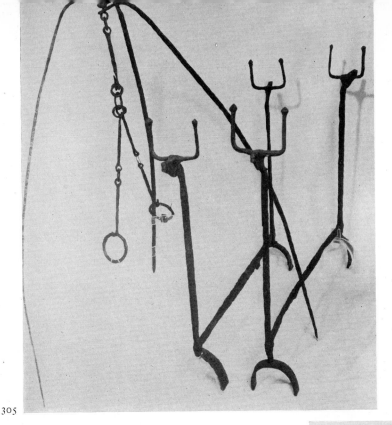

305

302 Grave goods from a female inhumation in a stone cist
(the local, native rite) at *Birdlip, Glos*. The rich equipment, including two bowls, a magnificently ornamented mirror and personal and costume jewellery,
indicates a lady of high rank. Maximum diam. of the
larger bowl 9 in.; the mirror weighs nearly $2\frac{1}{2}$ lbs.
First century AD. [CGM]

303 A bronze cup-handle with ox-head terminal from the
Birdlip burial; the eyes have lost their enamel or glass
inlay. Length about $2\frac{1}{2}$ in. [CGM]

304 The silver-gilt brooch from the *Birdlip* burial, with
zoomorphic ornament. It dates from the late first
century BC or early first AD. Length nearly $2\frac{1}{2}$ in.
[CGM]

305 Part of the 'kitchen' equipment from a paved 'vault'
burial at *Stanfordbury, Beds*. Besides these two pairs
of fire-dogs, tripod and cauldron (only the ring
handles survive), there were large wine jars, a bronze
wine jug and ladle, and imported pottery, etc., indicating a date soon after the Roman conquest. Wine
and the equipment for transporting, storing, mixing
and drinking it were among the main imports of the
Iron Age Britain. Fire-dogs just over 2 ft 6 in. tall.
[CMAE]

306 The ox-head terminals of fire-dogs from *Stanfordbury,
Beds*. and *Lord's Bridge, Cambs* (right). Note the
inlaid bronze eye in the former and the masterly
wrought-iron workmanship. First century AD. [CMAE]

306

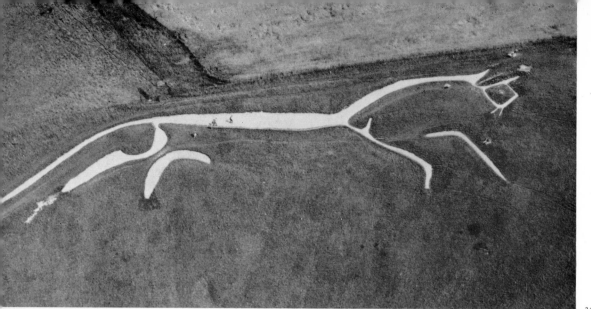

307 Chalk-cut figure of a horse on a hill-slope facing the Iron Age fort at *Uffington, Berks*, dated stylistically to the Iron Age (*cf* pls. 293, 299 and 311). Overall length about 120 yds. Maximum width of the outline about 10 ft

308 Detail of the eye and open lips of the *Uffington* horse; the eye is about 4 ft across on a levelled piece of ground; the outline may be cut down into the chalk to about 2 ft

309
310

311
312

309 Opposed 'sea-horses' on a stave-built tub from *Marlborough*, *Wilts*, with flying manes and delicately modelled heads. Horse-like figures, mythological beasts and gods are also known from parallels on the Continent and in Scandinavia. [DM]

310 Detail of one of the bronze hoops round the *Marlborough* tub, showing the full-face head, perhaps of a god, originally with inlaid eyes. Width of the hoop about 4 in. First century BC. [DM]

311 Tankard handle of native style but Roman date from *Silchester*, *Berks*. Compare with pls. 293 and 307. Length from muzzle to rear hoof about 4½ in. [RM]

312 Another detail from the *Marlborough* tub, the profile head, perhaps this time of a chief, with stylized hair, curving moustache, straight nose and almond-shaped eyes is typical of early Celtic art. [DM]

313

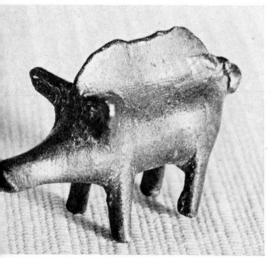

314

313 Figures of a boar, an indeterminate animal and a wheel from *Hounslow, Middlesex*. The boar occurs widely in ritual contexts (pig bones, for example, were buried with human remains in Yorkshire Iron Age burials), and the wheel is a common feature in Celtic iconography. Length of the boar 3¼ in. [BM]

314 Miniature figure of a boar found with an early type of Iron Age pin at *Woodendean, Brighton, Sussex*. Length 1½ in. [BRM]

315 Figure in the form of an ox head, possibly part of a handle-mount, from *Ham Hill, Somerset*, showing the delightful rendering of zoomorphic features in terms of Celtic art motifs. The occurrence of such heads in several different contexts (pls. 303, 306) suggests that the ox may have ritual importance. Length of head about 1¼ in. Late first century BC or early first century AD. [TM]

316 Handle-mount from *Boughton Aluph, Kent*, in the form of a face with eyes pierced for an inlay (*cf* pl. 310) and horns springing from the forehead. Possibly a representation of the Celtic horned god Cernunnos. Length 6½ in. First century BC. [MM]

316

317

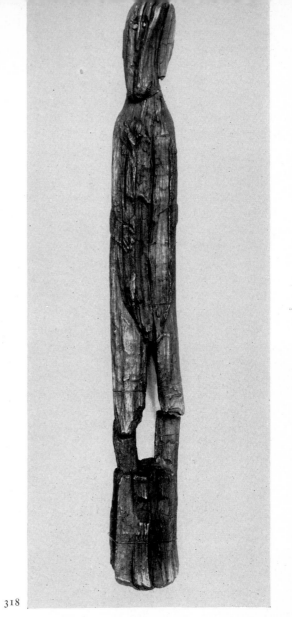

318

317 Wooden human figure from *Dagenham, Essex*, probably one of the tree-trunk idols of the Celtic world, in this case a male whose arms and phallus are now missing. Height 18 in. Possibly Iron Age. [CEM]

318 Wooden figure from *Ballachulish, Argyll*; this, unlike the Dagenham and Roos Carr figures, is a female, perhaps one of the Celtic fertility goddesses. Such an idol may have stood in the inner shrine of the Heathrow temple (pls. 225-6). This figure is large, standing about 5 ft tall. Possibly Iron Age. [NMAS]

319 The surviving remains of two boatloads of warriors from *Roos Carr, Yorks* (E.R.). Each would have carried a shield, the shape of which might suggest a later Bronze Age date for these models. Compare the form of the boat with pl. 196, and the idea of a ritual ship with pl. 156. Length of boat 20 in. Later Bronze Age or Iron Age. [HM]

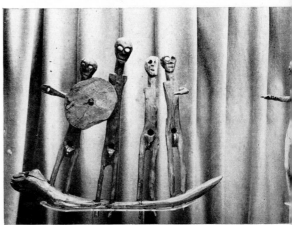

319

320

320 Close-up of one of the *Roos Carr* figures; the eyes
were inlaid with quartzite, as were the 'eyes' at the
prow of the boat; the face itself is strongly Celtic in
style. [HM]

Acknowledgements

Permission to reproduce plates has been given by institutions and individuals as follows (*the abbreviations are those used in the captions to the plates*):

R. D. Abbott 58

Aerofilms and Aeropictorial Ltd. 22, 110, 135, 278, 281, 307

P. Ashbee 46, 96, 162, 163, 166

By courtesy of the Ashmolean Museum, Oxford 118, 119, 134, 136, 186, 277, 282

R. J. C. Atkinson 97, 109, 121, 122, 128, 249, 250, 252, 253, 255, 256

Bath Academy of Art 143, 144

Cambridge University Copyright Reserved, photographs by J. K. St. Joseph, from the Cambridge University Collection, by permission of the Committee for Aerial Photography 7, 49, 279, 280

Cambridge University Museum of Archaeology and Ethnology 41, 42, 43, 44

Mrs Duncan Christie 168

City of Gloucester Museums (*CGM*) 302, 303, 304

City of Liverpool Museums (*CLM*) 76, 77, 242, 274

J. G. D. Clark 16

Copyright National Museum of Antiquities of Scotland (*NMAS*) 100, 318

J. X. W. P. Corcoran 139

Cornwall Archaeological Society 191

Crown Copyright Reserved, reproduced by permission of the Central Office of Information 187

Crown Copyright Reserved, photographs by J. K. St. Joseph, from the Cambridge University Collection, by permission of H.M. Ministry of Defence 52, 57, 65, 185

Crown Copyright Reserved, reproduced by permission of H.M. Ministry of Public Buildings and Works 32, 36, 46, 48, 54, 55, 59, 60, 61, 62, 66, 67, 68, 69, 72, 82, 83, 92, 93, 94, 96, 111, 112, 113, 114, 115, 120, 124, 133, 137, 138, 162, 163, 166, 221, 222, 223, 287, 288, 289, 290, 308

Crown Copyright Reserved, reproduced by permission of the Controller of H.M. Stationery Office 285

Dorset Natural History and Archaeological Society (*DCM*) 145

J. Ferrier 39

Glasgow Art Gallery and Museum (*GLM*) 131

W. F. Grimes 225, 226

Mrs C. M. Guido 190, 217, 218

D. W. Harding 216

Miss A. S. Henshall 71

G. A. Holleyman 188, 189

B. Hope-Taylor 180

Hull Museums (*HM*) 319

The Illustrated London News 180

G. Jobey 219, 232

Mrs G. Keiller 23

Miss K. M. Kenyon 290

W. Kirk 95

J. V. S. Megaw 300 and photograph on front of jacket

M. Murray 56, 87, 220

M. Murray and the National Museum of Antiquities of Scotland (*NMAS*) 21, 28, 29, 30, 45, 74, 84, 85, 86, 89, 130, 153, 154, 157, 159, 181, 196, 201, 202, 203, 205, 208, 210, 213, 248, 267, 272

National Museum of Wales, Cardiff (*NMW*) 8, 24, 34, 64, 156, 164, 167, 195, 243, 273, 275, 276, 286

Norwich Castle Museum (*NCM*) 247, 268

M. J. O'Kelly 73, 75

S. Piggott 94, 123

T. G. E. Powell 73, 75, 178, 179, 180, 242, 274

Prehistoric Society 41, 42, 43, 44, 76, 77, 94, 164, 178, 180, 188, 189, 197, 247, 268

Mrs E. V. W. Proudfoot 92, 93

Radio Times Hulton Picture Library 116
Royal Pavilion, Art Gallery and Museum, Brighton (*BRM*) 204

M. E. and J. G. Scott 70
Society of Antiquaries of London 50, 224, 283, 284
Society of Antiquaries of Newcastle upon Tyne 219, 232
Mrs J. F. S. Stone 51, 108

P. J. Tester 3
A. C. Thomas 191
N. de l'E. W. Thomas 137, 138
Trustees of the British Museum (*BM*) 13, 15, 88, 129, 178, 179, 251, 254, 259, 260, 261, 264, 299
Trustees of the British Museum (Natural History) (*BM(NH)*) 1
Trustees of the London Museum (*LM*) 165, 226, 246
Trustees of the National Maritime Museum (*NMM*) 198

University of Liverpool Press (reproduced from *Barclodiad y Gawres* by T. G. E. Powell and G. E. Daniel) 73, 75

Mrs F. de M. Vatcher 47, 48

Sir Mortimer Wheeler 50, 224, 283, 284
Douglas P. Wilson 117
Wiltshire Archaeological and Natural History Society Museum, Devizes (*DM*) 309, 310, 312
Charles Woolf 168
E. V. Wright 197

Permission was given for photographs to be taken specially for this book by the author as follows (*the abbreviations are those used in the captions to the plates*):

Avebury Museum (*AM*) 25, 31, 38

Brighton: Royal Pavilion, Art Gallery and Museum (*BRM*) 20, 141, 175, 194, 314
Bristol City Museum (*BCM*) 132, 183, 271

British Museum (*BM*) 37, 145, 149, 152, 155, 209, 211, 245, 298, 313

Cambridge University Museum of Archaeology and Ethnology (*CMAE*) 4, 17, 18, 19, 27, 35, 90, 91, 126, 151, 171, 172, 206, 291, 297, 305, 306
Cheddar: Gough's Cave Museum, by permission of the Marquess of Bath (*GCM*) 9, 10, 11, 12, 14
Colchester and Essex Museum (*CEM*) 182, 293, 294, 296, 301, 317

Devizes: Wiltshire Archaeological and Natural History Society Museum (*DM*) 53, 101, 102, 104, 105, 125, 140, 146, 147, 148, 150, 160, 161, 236, 237, 265, 292

Glastonbury: Glastonbury Antiquarian Society Museum (*GM*) 227, 230, 231, 241, 244

Hull Museums (*HM*) 320

Leicester City Museums and Art Gallery (*LEM*) 212
Lewes: Sussex Archaeological Society Museum (*SML*) 127, 192, 228, 229
London Museum (*LM*) 78, 79, 81, 106, 199, 200, 234, 257, 258, 295

Maidstone Museums and Art Gallery (*MM*) 2, 316

National Museum of Wales (*NMW*) 63, 107, 158, 170, 176, 214, 215, 233

Oxford: Ashmolean Museum (*AMO*) 26, 98, 99, 103, 174, 207, 263, 269

Reading Museum and Art Gallery (*RM*) 5, 6, 177, 262, 311

Salisbury, S. Wilts and Blackmore Museum (*SM*) 33, 80, 184, 193

Taunton: Somerset County Museum (*TM*) 173, 235, 238, 239, 240, 266, 270, 315

Worthing Museum and Art Gallery (*WM*) 169

Topographical index to plates

General index